MICHELANGELO

Drawings and Other Treasures
from the Casa Buonarroti, Florence

MICHELANGELO

Drawings and Other Treasures
from the Casa Buonarroti, Florence

Pina Ragionieri

Gary M. Radke, *Guest Curator*

Miranda MacPhail, *Translator*

HIGH MUSEUM OF ART

ATLANTA

Michelangelo: Drawings and Other Treasures from the Casa Buonarroti, Florence
This exhibition is organized by the High Museum of Art
in collaboration with the Casa Buonarroti, Florence.

In Atlanta, the exhibition is presented by by Northwestern Mutual Financial Networks.
Additional support is provided by Delta Air Lines and the Samuel H. Kress Foundation.

Michelangelo: Drawings and Other Treasures from the Casa Buonarroti, Florence
was on view at the
High Museum of Art, Atlanta, from June 23 to September 2, 2001
and at the
Toledo Museum of Art from September 21 to November 25, 2001.

Library of Congress Control Number: 00-136560
ISBN 0-939802-94-5

Cover: *Study for the Head of Leda,* circa 1530 (detail, cat. 8)
Frontispiece: *Madonna and Child,* circa 1525 (detail, cat. 7)
Page 6: Daniele da Volterra and Giambologna, *Bust of Michelangelo,*
head 1564–1566, bust circa 1570 (detail, cat. 2)

All photographs courtesy Casa Buonarroti, Florence.

For the High Museum of Art
Kelly Morris, Manager of Publications
Nora E. Poling, Associate Editor
Janet S. Rauscher, Assistant Editor
Melissa Duffes Wargo, Assistant Editor

Designed by Ed Marquand with assistance by Vivian Larkins
Produced by Marquand Books, Inc., Seattle
Printed by Amilcare Pizzi, Milan, Italy

CONTENTS

DIRECTOR'S PREFACE

HIGH MUSEUM OF ART

The High Museum of Art is privileged to introduce the American public to the artistic treasures of the Casa Buonarroti in Florence. The family home of Michelangelo Buonarroti—surely Italy's most famous artist—the Casa Buonarroti boasts the world's largest collection of Michelangelo's drawings and personal papers. Now a private foundation and museum, the Casa Buonarroti is also well known for art and antiquities collected by Michelangelo's family members. The exhibition provides a special opportunity for Americans to view works by and associated with one of the greatest artists in history, experiencing firsthand the rare drawings of the Renaissance master. The High will continue to engage in international partnerships to bring Europe's finest art to the Southeast.

In this exhibition, viewers will encounter works that for centuries were accessible only to intimate friends of the Buonarroti family. Even today, Michelangelo's drawings are usually kept in storage to protect them from exposure to damaging light and air. The vast majority of professional art historians and regular visitors to Florence have never seen these works.

By most counts, there are less than a dozen sheets of drawings by Michelangelo in American collections and no paintings or sculpture. Now another two dozen superb sketches and preparatory studies for such important works as the Sistine Chapel and the Medici tombs are visible in the United States. This exhibition affords an extraordinary view of Michelangelo through personal sketches, writings, and studies from the artist's notebooks, as well as insights into his family through painting, sculpture, and graphic works.

Some of my own favorite works in this exhibition include informal works such as a caricature Michelangelo made of himself painting the Sistine ceiling and another sheet from his notebooks containing tiny drawings of food for some of his meals. At the same time, who could not be in awe of his large, unfinished *Madonna and Child*? The nursing Christ Child seems to leap off the page as Michelangelo models the figure with warm chalk and white highlights. Equally impressive are his architectural plans. Included in this exhibition is the artist's largest surviving drawing for a building, the façade of the Florentine church of San Lorenzo, as well as working drawings and masterful sketches.

I trust that visitors to this exhibition will come away with a new appreciation for Michelangelo's art, his home, and his family. On behalf of all our friends at the Casa Buonarroti in Florence, I extend a heartfelt invitation to visit that museum when you are in Italy. It is located just one block away from the basilica of Santa Croce, where the famous artist worshipped, studied masterpieces of early Renaissance painting and sculpture, and was eventually buried.

Acknowledgments

Particular thanks are owed to Dr. Pina Ragionieri, the director of the Casa Buonarroti and author of this catalogue, and Dr. Gary M. Radke, the High Museum of Art's guest curator and professor of fine arts at Syracuse University, for their collaboration in shaping this exhibition for its American debut.

On our staff, the efficient and ebullient Julia Gómez, assistant to the deputy director and chief curator, oversaw the day-to-day development of the exhibition with good humor and patience. Jody Cohen, Manager of Exhibitions, and Exhibition Coordinators Linnea Harwell and Laurie Hicks were instrumental in seeing the project through to completion. David Brenneman, the Frances B. Bunzl Family Curator of European Art, and Phaedra Siebert, Curatorial Assistant in European Art, provided strong curatorial support. Kelly Morris, Nora Poling, Janet Rauscher, and Melissa Wargo, the High's tireless Publications team, have done a wonderful job of producing the English version of this catalogue.

As always, the entire staff of the High contributed their talents to make this exhibition and accompanying activities possible. Special thanks go to Philip Verre, Deputy Director; Rhonda Matheison, Director of Finance and Operations; Kevin Streiter, Manager of Museum Facilities; Charles Wilcoxson, Chief of Security; Marjorie Harvey, Director of Architectural Planning and Design; Jim Waters, Chief Preparator; Angela Jaeger, Head of Graphics; Maureen Morrisette, Associate Registrar; Kelly Ziegler, Exhibitions Assistant to the Registrar; H. Nichols B. Clark, Eleanor McDonald Storza Chair of Education; Joy Patty, Head of Adult Programs; Shantras Lakes, Head of Family and Community Programs; Pat Rodewald, Head of School Programs; Sheldon Wolf, Director of Museum Advancement; Nancy Gaddy, Manager of Corporate Support; Jennye Guy, Manager of Foundation and Government Support; Roanne Katcher, Manager of Membership; Dorie Wirtz, Manager of Volunteer Services; Sally Corbett, Manager of Communications; and Terry Williams, Manager of Special Events.

Delta Air Lines has provided funding to bring this exhibition to Atlanta. The Museum gratefully appreciates this generous support. Beginning with Samuel Kress's gift of a painting by Giambattista Tiepolo in 1932 and culminating with the gift of twenty-nine paintings and three sculptures in 1958, the Kress Foundation has played a pivotal role in the history of our institution. We thank them for their continuing generosity in helping to make this exhibition possible.

Michael E. Shapiro
Nancy and Holcombe T. Green, Jr. Director
HIGH MUSEUM OF ART

DIRECTOR'S PREFACE

THE TOLEDO MUSEUM OF ART

Michelangelo Buonarroti: what a magnificent artist to present to our visitors as part of the Toledo Museum of Art's centennial celebrations! We enthusiastically join Atlanta's High Museum of Art, the organizer of this exhibition, in offering the rare and wonderful treasures of the Casa Buonarroti to the American public.

All the works in this exhibition come from the Florentine residence that Michelangelo bought for his family in the early sixteenth century. Over the years, prominent family members renovated, enlarged, and decorated the Casa Buonarroti to serve as the appropriately grand setting for what was—and still is—the richest collection of Michelangelo's drawings and personal papers in the world. The Buonarroti also collected and commissioned other works of art that we are proud to feature in this exhibition alongside Michelangelo's magisterial drawings for the San Lorenzo complex in Florence and the Sistine Chapel in Rome.

Thanks to the diligent preservation of Michelangelo's papers by the Buonarroti family, viewers of this exhibition will be able to discover the private as well as the public Michelangelo. Pages from his hand-held notebooks show him drafting simple dinner menus complete with drawings of the food items, as well as providing instructions to the workmen who quarried his marble in Carrara. Michelangelo's supreme powers of invention are manifest in such drawings as his studies for the head of Leda and his designs for the New Sacristy in San Lorenzo. Notably, his handwriting appears regularly on these works, as do signs of his economy and practicality: he used many of the pages repeatedly, even over long periods of time. The entire spectrum of Michelangelo's genius—painting, sculpture, architecture, and poetry—is represented in these works on paper.

Acknowledgments

I am happy to take this occasion to thank the many colleagues who have helped us develop this project from its inception to its realization. First and foremost, Dr. Pina Ragioneri, director of the Casa Buonarroti and author of this catalogue, showed her generosity in making available the Casa Buonarroti treasures to an American public. Gary Radke, professor of fine arts at Syracuse University and guest curator for this exhibition, served as an invaluable liaison between Italy and America. Members of Toledo's staff, in particular Charlene Bettencourt, Giancarlo Fiorenza, Julie Mellby, Lawrence Nichols, and Mary Plouffe, all worked together to ensure the success of this exhibition. But most special thanks go to my colleague Michael Shapiro, director of the High, who brought this possibility to my attention and allowed us the opportunity to collaborate once again.

Roger M. Berkowitz

Director

THE TOLEDO MUSEUM OF ART

GUEST CURATOR'S PREFACE

Few families have done as much to preserve and promote the fame of an artist ancestor as the Buonarroti of Florence. They made their house—purchased for posterity by Michelangelo himself—into a shrine to art, learning, and the accomplishments of the "divine" Michelangelo.

This exhibition has been organized to allow visitors to meet key members of the artist's extraordinary family and encounter the more intimate side of Michelangelo's titanic genius. Here we see works that document family members' accomplishments as scholars, playwrights, and collectors. Michelangelo's personal notes and scribbles, masterful pen sketches, evocative chalk drawings, and precise architectural studies bring us extremely close to the man himself. These works concentrate all the power and intensity of Michelangelo's sculpture, painting, and architecture into accessible dimensions.

While the goal of this exhibition is to introduce Michelangelo's work to this community and to set it within the context of his family's intellectual and artistic accomplishments, it also provides important documentation of the artist's working methods. The drawings presented here range from just five inches long (a study of an arm for the Sistine ceiling) to more than three feet wide (a study on six sheets of paper for the façade of San Lorenzo in Florence). These are works that allow us to recognize and appreciate the challenges Michelangelo faced as he worked out his thoughts on paper. We literally catch the artist off guard as his hand responds to and shapes his thoughts. Michelangelo was often embarrassed by the hard mental and physical work that went into his creations, willfully destroying large groups of his drawings. Those that survive, some of which are presented in this exhibition, demonstrate how wrong he was to dismiss his preparatory work.

The exhibition includes examples of every major drawing medium in which the famous Florentine worked: charcoal, pen and ink, pen and wash, red chalk, and black chalk. A small wax model of a River God illustrates his "sketching" in three dimensions. The works range in function and purpose from preliminary ideas to much more finished works that Michelangelo intended to share with patrons and workmen. They testify both to his breadth of artistic activity and to his family's intelligent preservation of his works.

Acknowledgments

As guest curator, I have had the privilege of working closely with Dr. Pina Ragionieri, director of the Casa Buonarroti and author of this catalogue. It is her vision and research that determined the themes and organization of the exhibition as well as the specific content of the catalogue entries. She generously worked with me in developing the checklist for the exhibition, and her ideas and insights fully inform the wall text and labels I wrote for the installation.

I would like to thank the staffs of the Casa Buonarroti, the High Museum of Art, and the Toledo Museum of Art for all their kind cooperation, especially Dottoressa Elisabetta Archi in Florence, Julia Gómez, David Brenneman, Marge Harvey, Linnea Harwell, Laurie Hicks, Jody Cohen, and Kelly Morris in Atlanta, and Larry Nichols, Mary Plouffe, Julie Mellby, Giancarlo Fiorenza, and Roger Berkowitz in Toledo. It was a particular joy to work with Miranda MacPhail in Italy, who so thoughtfully translated the catalogue from Italian into English, and Elroy Quenroe, whose installation designs elegantly evoke Florence and the Casa Buonarroti. My greatest appreciation, however, goes to Michael E. Shapiro, Nancy and Holcombe T. Green, Jr. Director of the High Museum of Art, who asked me to join him on exploratory visits to museum officials in Florence and whose entrepreneurial and generous spirit made this exhibition a reality.

Gary M. Radke
Guest Curator

FOREWORD

Located in the center of Florence, Via Ghibellina is a historic street lined with ancient houses and palaces. Walking along it we find, at no. 70, a noble seventeenth-century building that by its very name evokes important and profound memories: the Casa Buonarroti. Housed behind its severe façade is an institution devoted to carrying out—on the local level, but also nationally and internationally—the role that its history imposes.

The most well-known expression of this is the Museum, which contains some of Michelangelo's masterpieces, including the two symbols of the Casa: the *Madonna of the Steps* and the *Battle of the Centaurs*. Both of these marble reliefs were created in Florence by the artist when he was barely a teenager. The first piece is vivid proof of his deep study of Donatello, while the second records his unwaning passion for classical art.

In addition, the Museum owns rich collections of paintings, sculptures, majolica ware, and archaeological pieces, acquired by various means over the generations of the Buonarroti family. The Museum also houses the most famous collection in the world of drawings by Michelangelo's own hand, as well as the inestimable papers from the centuries-old archive of the Buonarroti family.

Among the objectives of the present exhibition, the desire to promote the knowledge of this extraordinary heritage of memories and art works is especially significant. Through a selection of materials that allows us to "visit," albeit from afar, the ancient Florentine building, we can discover hidden aspects that evoke the Casa's old inhabitants. It is no accident that the first section of the exhibition is titled "Michelangelo and the Casa Buonarroti."

Our encounter with Michelangelo continues on through the two following sections. Here we explore salient moments in the human and artistic experience of this great genius: his troubled relationships with patrons, completed art works, and unfinished projects related to the building of the San Lorenzo complex in Florence; and the exalted but for the most part solitary venture of the Sistine Chapel.

Casa Buonarroti's relationship with Michelangelo and his myth runs deep and so long over time as to seem perpetual. For three centuries after the artist's death, while his direct descendents were still living in the Via Ghibellina building, the property's changing of hands never erased the artist's strong presence and memory. The continued projection, in changing situations, of his great shadow deeply impresses even today's visitors to the Casa and accompanies the institution's everyday work.

The Casa Buonarroti at the beginning of the nineteenth century

This is a necessary point of departure for understanding how this exhibition succeeds in tracing an intellectual, artistic, and human biography, drawing exclusively on art works belonging to the Casa Buonarroti. It also expresses the hope, for all those who accept this special invitation, that they will succeed in capturing the atmosphere and sensations that very much resemble those we experience upon entering no. 70 Via Ghibellina in Florence.

Acknowledgments

A special thanks to Giovanni Agosti and Luciano Berti for their friendly contribution of invaluable and constant support in the realization of the catalogue and the exhibition. We express our most sincere gratitude to Antonio Paolucci, Soprintendente per i Beni Artistici e Storici di Firenze, Prato e Pistoia (Superintendent of the Artistic and Historical Patrimony for Florence, Prato, and Pistoia), who has always supported and taken part in Casa Buonarroti's activity. Affectionate thanks go to Elisabetta Archi, Elena Lombardi, and Marcella Marongiu for their competent daily collaboration and to Stefano Corsi for his important assistance. The show benefited from the cheerful attention given by Maria Grazia Benini, Dirigente Superiore del Ministero per i Beni Culturali e Ambientali (Head Chief of the Ministry of Cultural and Environmental Patrimony), and by Pasquale Sassu, administrator of the Ente Casa Buonarroti accounts. Finally, our greatest thanks go to our friends at the High Museum of Art in Atlanta, especially Michael Shapiro and my guardian angel, Gary Radke, and to the wonderful staff of the Toledo Museum of Art, whose intelligent participation has allowed Casa Buonarroti's image to once more reach far-off lands.

Pina Ragionieri
Director
CASA BUONARROTI, FLORENCE

Michelangelo, *Madonna of the Steps*, Florence, Casa Buonarroti, inv. 190

Michelangelo, *Battle of the Centaurs*, Florence, Casa Buonarroti, inv. 194

MICHELANGELO
BUONARROTI

HIS LIFE AND WORKS

Michelangelo Buonarroti was born on March 6, 1475, in Caprese, a stony village not far from Arezzo in the Tuscan countryside, where his father was town governor. However, soon after his birth Michelangelo was taken to Florence, where he spent his boyhood and young adult years. The boy's gift for drawing showed itself at an early age and persuaded his father to apprentice him, in April 1487, to the workshop of the painter Domenico Ghirlandaio (1449–1494). However, the boy soon left his master to become a member of the "Garden of San Marco," which was supported by the Medici family. The Garden was a key part of the renowned patronage extended by Lorenzo de' Medici, also known as the Magnificent (1449–1492), Lord of Florence and a member of the city's most important family. In a wide open space of his property near the Piazza San Marco in Florence, Lorenzo had brought together ancient statues and art works with the aim of offering young artists the chance to learn and practice their craft, especially in sculpture, under the tutelage of Bertoldo di Giovanni (circa 1440–1491), an outstanding artist and a pupil of Donatello (1386–1466), the most important sculptor of the fifteenth century.

First welcomed into the Medici household under Lorenzo and then under his son Piero (1472–1503), Michelangelo created his first masterpieces during his studies at the Garden of San Marco, an experience that proved fundamental for his development. Today two of those masterpieces, the famous marble reliefs of the *Madonna of the Steps* and the *Battle of the Centaurs,* are still displayed in the Museum of the Casa Buonarroti. The mythological theme of the Battle had been suggested to the young artist by the humanist and man of letters Agnolo Poliziano (1454–1494).

After the deaths of Lorenzo the Magnificent and Agnolo Poliziano and faced with the prospect of Piero de' Medici's imminent exile from Florence, Michelangelo repaired first to Venice in 1494 and then to Bologna, where he stayed until the beginning of the following year. In Bologna he carried out several sculptures for the Arca di San Domenico, the saint's burial monument (located in the church of the same name), which had been under construction for more than two hundred years.

Upon his return to Florence, Michelangelo sculpted a *Sleeping Cupid* that was later sold without his knowledge by a dealer in Rome as a sculpture from classical antiquity unearthed during a dig. Soon, however, the real name of the artist behind the piece (one of Michelangelo's many lost works) was discovered, and the widespread admiration that resulted was the reason the young Florentine master was called to Rome.

During these first Roman years (1496–1501), Michelangelo carried out, among other works, the *Bacchus* (this statue of the Greco-Roman god is now preserved in the

Michelangelo, *Pietà*, Vatican City, St. Peter's

National Museum of the Bargello in Florence); the *Pietà* (the famous marble sculpture of the Madonna with the dead Christ that can still be seen in the basilica of Saint Peter in Rome); as well as several figures of saints for Cardinal Piccolomini's altar in the Siena cathedral.

When Michelangelo returned to Florence in 1501, he began work on the *David*, the colossal statue that would be placed in front of the Palazzo della Signoria in 1504. In 1503 he received a commission from the Opera del Duomo of Florence for twelve statues of the Apostles, but he only completed the *Saint Matthew* now displayed in the gallery of the Accademia in Florence.

In 1504 the artist began to work on the preparatory cartoon for the *Battle of Cascina*, a work that was to have been painted in the Great Council Hall (today known as the Salone dei Cinquecento) in Palazzo Vecchio, on the wall opposite the *Battle of Anghiari*, commissioned from Leonardo da Vinci (1452–1519). Neither of the two paintings was completed, and Michelangelo's composition never developed beyond the cartoon. This work is now lost, but at the time it was passionately studied,

Michelangelo, *Angel Holding a Candelabrum,*
Bologna, San Domenico

Michelangelo, *David* (detail), Florence,
Accademia Gallery

together with Leonardo's cartoon, by many young artists—and not only those from
Florence.

In these years, Michelangelo created three famous *tondi* ("rounds") portraying
the Madonna and Child: two in marble (the Pitti Tondo currently in the Bargello Museum and the Taddei Tondo now in the Royal Academy, London) and one painted
on a wood panel (the *Doni Tondo* in the Uffizi Gallery, Florence).

In 1505 Michelangelo left once more for Rome, called by Pope Julius II, who
wanted to engage the artist to carry out his funerary monument, which was to be built
in Saint Peter's at the Vatican. This was the beginning of a long and torturous business

Michelangelo, *Moses*, Rome, San Pietro in Vincoli

that the artist himself called "the tragedy of the tomb." Of the grandiose but never completed project only a few pieces remain: the male figures known as the *Prisoners* are found today in Paris at the Louvre and in Florence at the Accademia. Still others, with the famous statue of *Moses* at the center, were brought together by Michelangelo himself many years later, in 1545, in the Roman church of San Pietro in Vincoli.

In May 1508, the artist began the frescoes for the ceiling of the Sistine Chapel in the Vatican in Rome, an enormous undertaking, which he was to finish in October 1512. The impressive fresco cycle tells stories from the Bible, starting from the creation of the world, and the narrative scenes are flanked by monumental figures of Prophets and Sibyls.

In 1518, while he was still dividing his time between Rome and Florence, Michelangelo received the commission from Pope Leo X, Lorenzo the Magnificent's son, to construct and embellish with statues the façade of the Florentine church of San Lorenzo. The contract for this work was later rescinded, so the project was never carried out, but a large wooden model of Michelangelo's design still exists and can be seen at the Museum of the Casa Buonarroti. In 1519 the Pope ordered

Dome of the basilica of Saint Peter, Vatican City

Aerial view of the Piazza del Campidoglio, Rome

Michelangelo, *Rondanini Pietà*, Milan, Castello Sforzesco, Civic Art Collections

Michelangelo to erect a "New Sacristy" for the church of San Lorenzo, which was to serve as a burial chapel for the Medici family since there were no more spaces available in Brunelleschi's "Old Sacristy." Work on the Sacristy continued until 1534, following the wishes of the new Medici Pope Clement VII, who had in the meantime commissioned the artist to make the Laurentian Library, located in the same architectural complex, a project that was begun in 1524.

Between 1527 and 1530, Michelangelo passionately undertook his position as military architect in the defense of the Florentine Republic, which had come to power after the second expulsion of the Medici from rule of the city. In these years, tempestuous political events pushed him to seek occasional refuge in Ferrara and Venice. While he was working on the fortifications of Florence, he was simultaneously engaged in sculpting the Medici tombs in the New Sacristy.

In 1530, after the definitive return of the Medici to Florence, Michelangelo began to alternate presence in his native city with ever longer stays in Rome, where in 1532 he met the young Roman patrician Tommaso dei Cavalieri (circa 1511–1587), with whom he formed a deep friendship. This was one of the reasons why in 1534 he moved to Rome for good, staying in that city until his death and resisting the pressing invitations to return to Florence that were made to him over the years.

Still, the artist never gave up the affectionate ties with his family living in Florence. Until his death, he kept in constant communication with his nephew Leonardo (1519–1599), son of his brother Buonarroto (1477–1528). In the meantime, Michelangelo had accepted the commission to fresco the end wall of the Sistine Chapel, where he carried out *The Last Judgment* between 1534 and 1541.

It is in these years in Rome that his famous friendship with the poetess Vittoria Colonna (1492–1547) developed. Between 1541 and 1550, Michelangelo frescoed the Pauline Chapel in the Vatican with the *Martyrdom of Saint Peter* and the *Conversion of Saint Paul.*

In 1546 the artist undertook the completion of Palazzo Farnese, and the following year he was named architect of the basilica of Saint Peter; he held this position until his death and was strenuously engaged in constructing the new building and carrying out its great dome. Michelangelo's late works in Rome are in fact mostly architectural: the layout of the Piazza del Campidoglio and the renovation of the Church of Santa Maria degli Angeli. But he never abandoned his preferred art of sculpture; only a few days before he died he worked on his last *Pietà*, the unfinished *Rondanini Pietà*, now housed in the Castello Sforzesco in Milan. Michelangelo died on February 18, 1564.

Giuliano Finelli, *Portrait of Michelangelo Buonarroti the Younger*,
Florence, Casa Buonarroti, inv. 294

MICHELANGELO AND
THE CASA BUONARROTI

A bill of sale—an original document mentioned by Gaetano Milanesi in 1875 and published in 1965 by Ugo Procacci in his exhaustive catalogue of the Casa Buonarroti—proves that on March 3, 1508, Michelangelo bought, for the price of 1050 large florins, three houses and a small building in Florence, between Via Ghibellina and what is today Via Michelangelo Buonarroti. The artist bought another small house next door in April 1514. Of these five houses, three were probably rented out immediately. It is certain that Michelangelo lived with his family in the two more spacious buildings beginning in 1516—that is, when Medici commissions didn't force him to go looking for marble in Carrara or Pietrasanta. However, in 1525, under pressure from Pope Clement VII, he moved to the San Lorenzo quarter of Florence, where for years he had been engaged in works for the church façade, the New Sacristy, and the Laurentian Library. From that year on, the modest Via Ghibellina complex is documented as having been rented out entirely.

Michelangelo lived elsewhere, and yet a constant, even obsessive desire can be read in his papers, especially after his final move to Rome in 1534. Even more than a desire, it was the will to give, for all time to come, his family's name to a building in Florence, to what he called an "honorable house in the city." The family's only male heir, Leonardo (1519–1599), son of Michelangelo's brother Buonarroto, was only able to evade his important uncle's continuous exhortations by marrying Cassandra Ridolfi in 1553 and consenting to a renovation of the Via Ghibellina houses, albeit limited to only part of the property. Not much was accomplished during Michelangelo's lifetime, and it wasn't until 1590 that Leonardo's discontinuous interest turned at last to the family home to which Michelangelo had so long aspired.

However, the home would undergo its most significant phase of development under one of Leonardo's sons, Michelangelo Buonarroti the Younger (1568–1647). A noteworthy figure in Florentine culture during the first half of the seventeenth century, to date he has been studied more for his written works—he was a man of the theater and author of two famous plays, *La Tancia* and *La Fiera*—than for his exceptional talent as a versatile and enterprising cultural organizer, a friend and generous host of artists and scholars. The many volumes of his papers, dealing with the administration of his household and other writings, are conserved in the Archivio Buonarroti and are in large part still unpublished. Studying them could well reveal an interesting intellectual portrait, which until now has only been glimpsed.

Michelangelo the Younger added to the family real estate, and it was by his wishes that, between 1612 and 1640, the building assumed the features it still presents today, and not only externally. We can ascribe to him the realization of the monumental rooms on the second floor of the house that glorify his ancestor and

Gallery, Florence, Casa Buonarroti

exalt the family's greatness. Here the art of the Florentine and Tuscan Seicento reaches some of its greatest moments.

Michelangelo the Younger elaborated and personally oversaw the rooms' complex decorative program. He took such detailed notes on the relative events, payments, and dates that today there can be no doubt as to the authors of the works or the amount of time in which they carried out their pieces. The grandiose realization is further documented by numerous accounts from different sources, including a great-grandson of the same name, who wrote down the late-seventeenth-century inventory known as the "Descrizione buonarrotiana."

The most important artists in Florence at that time were called upon to work at the Casa. In these rooms, which have remained miraculously intact throughout the not infrequent contingencies and the sometimes heavy renovation undergone over time, the visitor can still view today a sampling of the greatest seventeenth-century Florentine and Tuscan art.

The first room, called the "Gallery" and set up between 1613 and 1635, takes as its theme the glory of Michelangelo the Artist, Man, and Poet, developing it into a singular biography through images. Here the place of honor used to be held by that extraordinary marble relief that Michelangelo had sculpted when, not yet sixteen years old, he was still studying under Bertoldo di Giovanni in the Garden of San Marco: the *Battle of the Centaurs,* which is still an emblematic work of the Casa and its Museum. The relief remained here until 1875, displayed under a large work that Michelangelo the Younger had acquired, believing it was made by his great ancestor's hand. The painting, however, though it is based on Michelangelo's cartoon, was later found to have been executed by the master's pupil and biographer Ascanio Condivi (circa 1525–1574).

Giovanni di Francesco, *Scenes of Saint Nicholas of Bari* (detail), Florence, Casa Buonarroti, inv. 68

Room of Night and Day, Florence, Casa Buonarroti

The decoration of the second room, the "Room of Night and Day," was begun in 1624 and continued for years. In 1625 Jacopo Vignali painted the ceiling fresco *God the Father Dividing the Light from the Darkness* as well as the personifications of Night and Day for which the room is named. Here the most unusual characteristic is the small chamber adorned by pleasant frescoes and closed by doors as if it were a wardrobe; this is the "Writing Cabinet," where Michelangelo the Younger used to retire to study.

The fresco decoration continues along the walls with the portraits of family figures. The room is also adorned by such important art works as *Scenes of Saint Nicholas of Bari*, a masterpiece by Giovanni di Francesco, a painter active in Florence around the mid-fifteenth century; the famous portrait of Michelangelo by Giuliano Bugiardini; and the bronze head of the artist by Daniele da Volterra.

Room of the Angels, Florence, Casa Buonarroti

The itinerary continues with the "Room of the Angels," which was used as a chapel from 1677 on. The wall frescoes by Jacopo Vignali show the figures of saints marching in procession from the Militant Church toward the Triumphant Church. Upon entering the room, one can't help admiring, above the altar, the great inlaid woodwork of the *Madonna and Child,* based on a cartoon by Pietro da Cortona and dating from about 1642. (Some of the doors on the Casa's second floor have precious inlays based on more cartoons by the same artist, who was the proprietor's friend and houseguest during the years spent in Florence working at Palazzo Pitti.) The same room hosts the famous marble bust of Michelangelo the Younger by Giuliano Finelli, a pupil of Bernini.

In the fourth room, the "Study," the interior decoration dates from the years 1633–1637. High on the walls appear depictions of illustrious Tuscans painted by Cecco Bravo, Matteo Rosselli, and Domenico Pugliani in a picturesque succession of faithfully illustrated well-known likenesses. A series of wooden wardrobes, with inlays in ivory and mother-of-pearl, runs along the walls under the frescoes, interspersed with display cases in which one can see different aspects of the family's collecting.

The four large rooms, followed by a small chamber where Michelangelo the Younger liked to crowd the many pieces of his collections, have remained intact over the centuries and so constitute a unique case in contrast to the Casa's other less fortunate interior rooms. For instance, an early nineteenth-century renovation almost completely erased one of Michelangelo the Younger's contributions located near the attic loggia: a sort of hanging garden of delights, resembling a grotto with stucco decorations, artificial sponge formations, and plays of water. The only thing that

Benedetto Calenzuoli, based on a cartoon by Pietro da Cortona, *Madonna and Child,*
Florence, Casa Buonarroti, inv. 398

Study, Florence, Casa Buonarroti

Francesco Montelatici, called "Cecco Bravo," *Fame,* Florence, Casa Buonarroti, inv. 502

Michelangelo, *Two Combatants*, Florence, Casa Buonarroti, inv. 192

remains of all this is a room (next to the still-existing roof belvedere), restored in 1964 but unfortunately difficult to get to and so not included in the visitors' tour of the Museum. The room's ceiling was pleasantly decorated by Giovan Battista Cartei, who painted the frescoes in 1638, showing trellis-work crossed by birds in flight.

Two of Michelangelo the Younger's essential traits—his passion for collecting and his cultivation of the family's memory—were fundamental in the formation of the family's artistic legacy. To him goes the merit of having bought ancient sculpture; it was he who wanted to place the *Battle of the Centaurs* in its preeminent position in the first monumental room; it was he who contracted with the sacristan of Santa Croce to buy the predella of the *Stories of Saint Nicholas;* to him Casa Buonarroti owes the recovery of the marble relief known as the *Madonna of the Steps,* not to mention many drawings by Michelangelo's hand.

And here it would be best to pause for a moment and turn back in time to talk about what is perhaps the Casa's most precious treasure: the collection of Michelangelo's drawings.

Michelangelo's most famous biographer, the painter and architect Giorgio Vasari (1511–1574), in writing about the artist's desire for perfection, tells that, before his death in Rome in 1564, Michelangelo wanted to burn "a large number of drawings, sketches, and cartoons made by his own hand so that no one would see the labor

Michelangelo, *Cleopatra*, Florence, Casa Buonarroti, inv. 2F recto

Michelangelo, *Cleopatra*, Florence, Casa Buonarroti, inv. 2F verso

Michelangelo, *Plan for the Church of San Giovanni dei Fiorentini,*
Florence, Casa Buonarroti, inv. 124A

he went through and the ways in which his genius made its attempts, in order not to appear anything but perfect." By good luck, a number of Michelangelo's drawings were still in Florence at the time of his death and others were recovered in Rome by his nephew Leonardo. The latter, however, in order to satisfy the collector and Duke of Tuscany Cosimo I de' Medici (1519–1574), gave him a good number of these drawings after the death of his uncle and before 1568. Into the same hands he also gave the *Madonna of the Steps* and everything that had been left behind in the Florentine studio when Michelangelo moved to Rome for good.

As we have seen, more than fifty years later, Michelangelo the Younger set up a series of rooms in the family house in honor of his ancestor's memory. At that time the *Madonna of the Steps* and part of the drawings given to the Medici were returned to him by Duke Cosimo II (1590–1621), and the respectful great-nephew went about recovering at a dear price—on the Roman market, too—more drawings by Michelangelo's hand. Most of the drawings were then compiled in bound volumes, but the most beautiful ones were framed and hung on the walls of the new rooms.

The Buonarroti family collection was, at that point, the largest collection of Michelangelo's drawings in the world. And, with its more than two hundred works, this still holds true today, in spite of the serious attempts at division that it has suffered. Diminished at the end of the eighteenth century by a first sale that the family revolutionary Filippo Buonarroti (1761–1837) made to French painter and collector Jean Baptiste Wicar (1762–1834) in October of 1858, the collection underwent a further serious reduction when Cavalier Michelangelo Buonarroti sold more drawings to the British Museum.

The last direct heir to the family, Cosimo Buonarroti (born in 1790), also owned the greatest number of Michelangelo's papers. A few months before he died, he wrote in his will that these, together with the palazzo in Via Ghibellina and its contents, were to be left for public enjoyment.

After that time, the precious drawings remained on exhibit in frames and display cases for many years. It wasn't until 1960 that they were saved from this risky way of keeping them, which at times had damaged their state of conservation. Taken to the Uffizi Cabinet of Drawings and Engravings, where they were restored, the drawings did not return to the Casa Buonarroti until 1975. Currently they are displayed, on a rotational basis, in a room in the Museum that has been set up with correct lighting levels and controlled humidity conditions.

But let's go back to the history of the Buonarroti family and their home. Michelangelo the Younger died in 1647 and, as Filippo Baldinucci (the Florentine memorialist and man of letters) wrote, he was mourned "not only by all the virtuous men but also by the whole city, to whom his rare qualities were well known." He was succeeded in overseeing the Casa by his nephew Leonardo, who proved a magnanimous custodian of the property. In turn, Leonardo ensured the property's integral preservation through the ironclad clauses of his will. At his death, the house passed into the hands of his son Michelangelo, the probable author of the aforementioned *Descrizione buonarrotiana*.

Next in succession—already at the beginning of the eighteenth century—the property came to Filippo Buonarroti (1661–1733), not by right of primogeniture but because of his great reputation as an antiquarian and important archaeologist. He enriched the family collections with Etruscan and Roman works, which for the last four years have been on display in the Museum and of which an eloquent sampling is included in the present exhibition. Under Filippo's supervision, the Casa went back to hosting illustrious visitors, as in the times of Michelangelo the Younger, and it lived its period of greatest splendor.

But there were difficult years ahead, both for the building and the family, during the eighteenth and nineteenth centuries. In 1799 the Austrian forces occupying Florence ordered that the Buonarroti patrimony be confiscated and assigned to the Hospital of Santa Maria Nuova. This was because, at the time, the legitimate heir—the famous Filippo (1761–1837),

Stele of Larth Ninie, Florence, Casa Buonarroti, inv. 54

Portrait of Filippo Buonarroti (1761–1837),
Florence, Casa Buonarroti

a revolutionary and follower of Robespierre, living for years in exile in France—was awaiting deportation for having participated in the 1796 conspiracy of Babeuf's Society of Equals.

In all probability, Filippo's shrewd wife is to thank for having the property assigned once more to the family. In 1812 Filippo's son, Cosimo Buonarroti (1790–1858), future Minister of Public Education during the Grand Duke's reign in Tuscany, succeeded in regaining possession of the house in Via Ghibellina. At that time the house was rather run-down: a report of June 10, 1823, filed by an inspector to document the improvements that Cosimo had already carried out, reads that "the Buonarroti house in Via Ghibellina in 1820 had become almost a hovel for the most abject class of the population." After making some important restorations, Cosimo took up residence in the Casa. In 1846 he married the Anglo-Venetian noblewoman Rosina Vendramin (1814–1856) and devoted himself with great passion to his family's history.

In his will, Cosimo left the Via Ghibellina building and all its precious contents for public enjoyment. At his death, since there were no direct heirs, the Casa passed to the City of Florence but only after bitter protests on the part of the indirect heirs. One year later the Casa Buonarroti was founded as an officially recognized institution by decree of Grand Duke Leopold II.

The institution's management of the Casa was first seen most visibly during the celebrations of the four-hundredth anniversary of Michelangelo's birth that took place in Florence in 1875. The Casa Buonarroti still preserves a great deal of documentation about these events, collected and displayed in two rooms of the Museum. The anniversary celebration was to have enduring repercussions on the city's customs and cultural life, from the laying out of Piazzale Michelangelo to the design of the Tribune for the *David* in the Galleria dell'Accademia. At the time there had also been the idea of adorning the façade of the Via Ghibellina building with a complex graffito decoration of which the large preparatory drawing still exists today. However, financial problems became so pressing that many areas of the palazzo had to be rented out as private homes, and in 1881 the decision was made to transfer the antiquity collections to the Archaeological Museum, where they remained for more than a century. At the beginning of the twentieth century, the Casa hosted the Historical and Topographical Museum of Florence; after the First World War, it went back to being divided up and partially rented out. The first modern restorations date to 1951,

Aristodemo Costoli, *Portrait of Cosimo Buonarroti*,
Florence, Casa Buonarroti, inv. 1

Aristodemo Costoli, *Portrait of Rosina
Vendramin*, Florence, Casa Buonarroti, inv. 3

Unknown Artist of the Nineteenth Century, *Casa Buonarroti,* Florence,
Casa Buonarroti, inv. 554

carried out in honor of Giovanni Poggi (1880–1961), the Michelangelo scholar who
had ensured that many works from the Florentine galleries would be deposited at the
Casa Buonarroti.

Right after the four-hundredth anniversary of Michelangelo's death (1964), the
Ente Casa Buonarroti was constituted by State law and Charles de Tolnay became the
director. The Hungarian scholar was called to Florence from Princeton after he had
already produced his well-known and monumental monograph on Michelangelo.
Tolnay stayed on as director of the Ente until his death in 1981, continuing his studies of Michelangelo's drawings, reordering the collections, and enriching the library
with important works.

A noteworthy consequence of the 1964 celebrations was the acquisition by Casa
Buonarroti, from the Accademia delle Arti del Disegno (Academy of the Arts of
Design), of the only Michelangelesque model of large dimensions, the *River God,*
an exciting work that can be admired today in the Museum, next to the wooden
model of the San Lorenzo façade.

This brings us to the present directorship, which—with the enlightened help
and consensus of a strongly participating Board of Administration presided over by
two distinguished Michelangelo scholars (first Paola Barocchi and, since 1991, Luciano
Berti)—has for many years undertaken a critical reappraisal of the institution's
history. It is precisely this objective that drives the institution's whole activity, in
this Home which is not just a Museum but also a place of study and research, with
an important library open for consultation by scholars and specializing in
Michelangelesque bibliography. We carry out our job in an institution in which we
not only reflect on past events but also oversee the conservation of this artistic patrimony and try, through different kinds of programming, to promote knowledge of the
structure elsewhere.

Amos Cassioli, Federigo Andreotti, Niccolò Barabino, Cosimo Conti, Corinto Corinti, Giacomo Roster, *Project for Incised Decoration for the Façade of the Casa Buonarroti*, Florence, Casa Buonarroti, inv. 667

The collaboration with Italian and foreign scholars of different generations, the continuing relationship with national and international institutions, the daily tasks involving Michelangelo's papers and works, the annual schedule of exhibitions—all constitute the basis of our work. In recent years, it has brought us to examine such unusual subjects as the comparative study of Michelangelo's life and handwriting, and the reexamination of the artist's tormented relationship with the building projects of Saint Peter's and San Lorenzo. This latter theme constitutes a large part of the present exhibition.

1.

CAFAGGIOLO WORKSHOP

Plate with the Buonarroti Coat of Arms, mid-sixteenth century
Majolica, 10⅞ inches in diameter
inv. 79

At the center of this plate are the Buonarroti family arms, which include the emblems of the Medici Pope Leo X. The Pope had granted their use to Michelangelo's brother, Buonarroto Buonarroti, when he was appointed prior in 1515; on that occasion, the Pope decreed that priors in office could use the blue Medici ball with the French fleur-de-lis and the letters "L.P.X." (Leo Pontifex X) in their family coats of arms. The Buonarroti arms incorporated these emblems from that moment on. The episode is represented in a fresco by Pietro da Cortona in the Room of Night and Day, the second of the seventeenth-century rooms in the Casa Buonarroti. The plate was made in the celebrated majolica workshop of Cafaggiolo in the Mugello area near Florence, a manufactory established in the late fifteenth century in the Medici castle of the same name. On the back, the faded "SPR" can still be seen, the mark that identified Cafaggiolo production for about a hundred years.

Pietro da Cortona, *Leo X names Buonarroto Buonarroti a Palatine Count*,
Florence, Casa Buonarroti, inv. 290

Alessandro Alinari, in *Ceramica toscana dal Medioevo al XVIII secolo*, edited by Gian Carlo Boiani, exhibition cat., Rome 1990, pp. 159–160.

2.

DANIELE DA VOLTERRA (1509–1566) and
GIAMBOLOGNA (1529–1608)

> *Bust of Michelangelo*, head 1564–1566, bust circa 1570
> Bronze, 23¼ inches high
> inv. 61

U pon Michelangelo's death in 1564, Daniele da Volterra used the death mask to make a portrait of the artist, with whom he had formed an intense friendship. When Daniele died two years later, six bronze heads of Michelangelo were found in his workshop. Two of them, which had not yet been sufficiently finished, went to Leonardo Buonarroti, the artist's nephew. Soon after the heads arrived in Florence, one of them disappeared without a trace, while the other was elaborated with a rich mantle cast by Giambologna. The involvement of the great Flemish sculptor led to his being named, in the Descrizione buonarrotiana, as the artist of the whole bust.

Jacopino del Conte, *Portrait of Michelangelo*, Florence, Casa Buonarroti, inv. Gallerie 1890, n. 1708

In 1767 Leonardo Buonarroti, then owner of the Casa, presented the work attributed to Giambologna at the exhibition held in the cloister of the Santissima Annunziata, where the most important Florentine families showed their treasures. The Buonarroti family also displayed two of Michelangelo's works: a "low relief in marble" and a "woman's head drawn in black pencil" (perhaps the *Cleopatra*), as well as the *Head of an Old Man* traditionally attributed to Guido Reni. The Casa Buonarroti bronze is considered, both for its history and for its quality, one of the most important examples of this famous sculptural portrait of Michelangelo. In the Casa Buonarrotti, it is displayed on its original seventeenth-century wooden pedestal, listed in the Descrizione buonarrotiana.

BIBLIOGRAPHY

Fabia Borroni Salvadori, "Le esposizioni d'arte a Firenze dal 1674 al 1767," in *Mitteilungen des Kunsthistorischen Institutes in Florenz*, XVIII, 1974, pp. 70, 90, 115, 140.

Alessandro Cecchi, in Henry A. Millon and Vittorio Magnago Lampugnani, *Rinascimento da Brunelleschi a Michelangelo. La rappresentazione dell'architettura*, exhibition cat., Milan 1994, pp. 658–659, no. 385.

Eika Schmidt, in *Vittoria Colonna Dichterin und Muse Michelangelos*, edited by Sylvia Ferino-Padgen, exhibition cat., Vienna 1997, pp. 314–316, no. IV.1.

3.

LEONE LEONI (1509–1590)
Medal of Michelangelo, 1561
Lead, 2½ inches in diameter
inv. 611

On March 14, 1561, Leone Leoni sent Michelangelo a letter along with four exemplars of the famous and beautiful medal that he had devoted to the Florentine master. (Modeled in Rome and cast in Milan, there were two medals in silver and two in bronze.) From another letter sent to Michelangelo about one month later we learn that Leoni was still waiting, and with a certain degree of anxiety, for confirmation of their receipt.

The medal was extolled a few years later by Vasari, in his *Life of Michelangelo*, with these words: "And at that time the Cavalier Lione portrayed Michelangelo very vivaciously in a medal, and to his pleasure made him on the back a blind man led by a dog . . . and because he liked it well, Michelangelo gave him a wax model of a Hercules and Anteus, in his own hand, and several of his drawings."

The recto of this medal bears a bust of Michelangelo viewed in profile facing right. The words "MICHELANGELUS BONARROTUS FLOR(entinus) AET(atis) S(uae) ANN(is) 88" appear around the edge. The indication of the age is clearly wrong, as Michelangelo was born in 1475. At the base of the bust is the artist's signature ("LEO"). On the verso appears an elderly blind man with Michelangelo's features, led by a dog. The legend around the edge, "DOCEBO INIQUOS V(ias) T(uas) ET IMPII AD TE CONVER(tentur)," is taken from Psalms 51:15.

Leone Leoni, Casa degli Omenoni, Milan

The meaning of Michelangelo's portrait as a blind man is still the subject of much debate. It might be worthwhile accepting the least far-fetched interpretation, which recognizes in it a symbol of earthly pilgrimage. It should be noted that the description of this verso contained in Giovanni Paolo Lomazzo's *Trattato dell'arte de la pittura, scoltura et architettura* (*Treatise on the Art of Painting, Sculpture, and Architecture*, 1584) differs from the examples known today in the detail of the dog's taut leash: "a medal of a fine statue, and on the back from where he had portrayed Michelangelo, he had made a poor man led by a dog tied with a cord around his neck which was pulled tight and straight like a stick, without any slack; which gave occasion for even a child to make fun of it and say that, if the dog had really pulled the cord so strongly, he would either have choked or he wouldn't have been able to go on; with so much laughter that several painters who were there with me were ready to burst."

As we have seen, Leone Leoni's gift to Michelangelo included four pieces, two in silver and two in bronze. Therefore the exemplar in lead, on display here, cannot be counted as one of these. From a technical point of view, it could constitute an "artist's proof"; on the other hand, the existence of sixteenth-century lead casts of this medal is attested by the "rather large lead impressions with the images of various famous men" (among them Michelangelo) in the late-sixteenth-century collection of Antonio Giganti, a cleric at the service of prelates and cardinals, the inventory of which was made known by Gigliola Fragnito.

Pollard suggests that, given its extraordinary quality, the silver medal now preserved in the Bargello Museum in Florence came to the Medici collections through a direct acquisition from the Buonarroti family. In his March 14 letter, Leone Leoni

Leone Leoni, Monument to Gian Giacomo de' Medici, Milan, Cathedral

alluded to a papal commission received through Michelangelo's good offices, a commission that had delayed his sending the medals. The project, for which he signed a contract on September 12, 1560, was the tomb of Gian Giacomo de' Medici, Marquis of Marignano, brother of Pius IV. According to Vasari, Leone Leoni used a drawing given him by Michelangelo for the grandiose monument, and the work was placed in the right-hand transept of the Duomo in Milan, where it can still be seen today. It is one of the main testaments to the great name that Leone Leoni achieved in Milan; his fame allowed him to build a spectacular home, the so-called Casa degli Omenoni, where Vasari was a guest during his 1566 stay in the city.

BIBLIOGRAPHY

J. Graham Pollard, "Il medagliere mediceo," in *Gli Uffizi. Quattro secoli di una galleria*, edited by Paola Barocchi and Giovanna Ragionieri, Florence 1983, p. 281.

——, *Medaglie italiane del Rinascimento nel Museo Nazionale del Bargello*, III, Florence 1985, pp. 1234–1236, no. 719.

Gigliola Fragnito, *In museo e in villa. Saggi sul Rinascimento perduto*, Venice 1988, p. 194.

Philip Attwood, in *The Currency of Fame: Portrait Medals of the Renaissance*, edited by Stephen K. Scher, exhibition cat., New York 1994, pp. 155–157, no. 52.

4.

SIXTEENTH-CENTURY ARTIST
Madonna of the Steps (after Michelangelo), circa 1566
Bronze, 22½ x 15¾ inches
inv. 531

This bronze relief reproduces Michelangelo's marble *Madonna of the Steps*, one of the youthful masterpieces housed in the Casa Buonarroti Museum. The marble work, made by the adolescent artist around 1490, remained in the Via Ghibellina house until Michelangelo's nephew Leonardo, after the death of his uncle and before 1568, gave it as a gift to Duke Cosimo I de' Medici. The bronze casting was in all likelihood made on that occasion. The oldest evidence of the work dates from the late seventeenth century when, in the inventory known as the Descrizione buonarrotiana, it is mentioned as occupying a niche in the Room of the Angels, where it has recently been placed once again. The same room displayed the master's marble relief after Cosimo II returned it to Michelangelo Buonarroti the Younger in 1616. The bronze relief, which still bears its original frame, has traditionally but erroneously been attributed to Giambologna. More recently it has been ascribed—but this proposal also seems unconvincing—to Vincenzo Danti.

BIBLIOGRAPHY

Hellmut Wohl, "Two Cinquecento Puzzles," in *Antichità viva*, XXX, 1991, pp. 42–48, no. 6.
Giovan Battista Fidanza, *Vincenzo Danti 1530–1576*, Florence 1996, p. 112.

5.

MICHELANGELO

Nude Seen from Behind, circa 1504–1505
Pen and traces of black pencil on paper, 16⅛ x 11¼ inches
inv. 73F

This drawing, one of the most well known and most published of the Casa Buonarroti Collection, has been identified as a study for the central group of young bathers in the *Battle of Cascina.* The fresco was commissioned from Michelangelo, probably in 1504, by the Florentine City Council for the Sala del Maggior Consiglio (today the Salone dei Cinquecento) in the Palazzo Vecchio, where Leonardo was to paint, in competition, the *Battle of Anghiari.* As is commonly known, neither of the works was ever finished.

Sheet 613E in the Uffizi's Cabinet of Drawings and Prints contains a sketch for the fresco's composition and shows this figure in the group of male nudes running toward the background on the left. From the copy of the cartoon for the *Battle of Cascina* made in monochrome on panel by Aristotele da Sangallo in 1542 (now in Holkham Hall), we can deduce that Michelangelo omitted this figure in a later elaboration of the project.

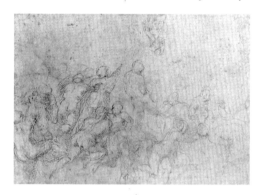

Michelangelo, *Study of the Left Part of the "Battle of Cascina,"* Florence, Cabinet of Drawings and Prints, Uffizi Gallery, inv. 613E

Aristotele da Sangallo, *Battle of Cascina* (after Michelangelo), Norfolk, Holkham Hall, Leicester Collection

Wilde first hypothesized this drawing's reference to antiquity and likened its composition to the figures on a late Roman sarcophagus showing the Labors of Hercules. This indication, which the same author defined as "generic," nevertheless represents one point along the long line that, over Michelangelo's artistic career, shows his constant relationship with antiquity.

More than twenty years later, between September and October of 1528, Michelangelo reused this paper, after having folded it in four, to take some notes regarding his nephew Leonardo (the payment for making a cloak and a pair of shoes for him on one of his visits) as well as jotting down other small expenses.

BIBLIOGRAPHY

Johannes Wilde, "Eine Studie Michelangelos nach der Antike," in *Mitteilungen des Kunsthistorischen Institutes in Florenz,* IV, 1932–1934, pp. 41–64.

Giovanni Agosti and Vincenzo Farinella, *Michelangelo e l'arte classica,* exhibition cat., Casa Buonarroti, Florence 1987, pp. 35–36, no. 9.

Michael Hirst, *Michel-Ange dessinateur,* exhibition cat., Paris and Milan 1989, pp. 16–17, no. 5.

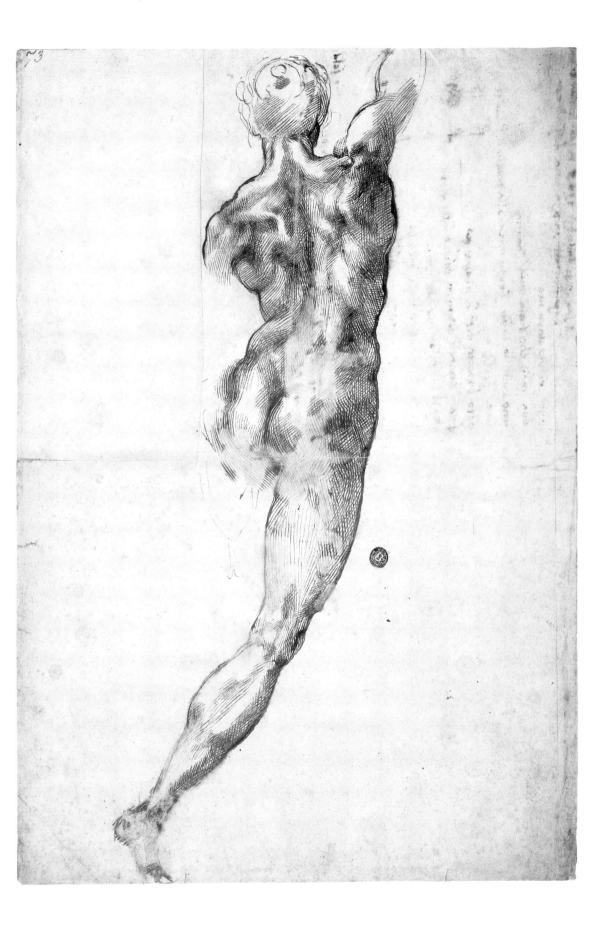

6.

MICHELANGELO

Three Different Lists of Foods, 1518
Pen and ink on paper, 8⅜ x 5¾ inches
Archivio Buonarroti, vol. X, f.578 verso

While Michelangelo was quarrying marble in Pietrasanta, he jotted down these three menus for three different kinds of meals on the back of a letter that had been sent to him on March 18, 1518, by Bernardo Nicolini. In other words, he used—as he often did, since it was his custom not to waste paper—the first sheet of paper that came to hand. Moreover, the food list, which describes an essential menu for two, four, or six people, shows his scrupulousness in recording the expenses and events of his day-to-day life. It testifies to Michelangelo's frugal way of living, which has often been pointed out by his biographers. The "bochal di tondo" in the last line seems to allow each of the six diners a glass of wine from the Colle Tondo, near Serravezza and not far from Pietrasanta.

The note in this case might have been made by the sculptor Pietro Urbano, one of the artist's collaborators. In fact, Michelangelo's administrative papers from this period often include notes in Pietro Urbano's handwriting regarding everyday expenses. On the other hand, the strength and confidence of the handwriting make even these utilitarian notes a typical manifestation of a great artist's genius.

The other annotations say: "Two rolls, a pitcher of wine, a herring; tortelli; a salad, four rolls, a pitcher of wine, a small quarter of a rough wine, a plate of spinach, four anchovies, tortelli; six rolls, two fennel soups, a herring, a pitcher of wine."

BIBLIOGRAPHY

Lucilla Bardeschi Ciulich, *Costanza ed evoluzione nella scrittura di Michelangelo,* exhibition cat., Casa Buonarroti, Florence 1989, pp. 28–29, no. 10.

———, *Michelangelo. Grafia e biografia di un genio,* exhibition cat., Milan 2000, p. 44.

pani dua
u bochal di vino
una aringa
tortegli

una salata
e quatro pani
u bochal del tondo
un quartuccio di bruscho
un pianello di spinaci
quatro a li ci
tortelli

sei pani
dua minestre di finochio
una aringa
u bochal di tondo

7

MICHELANGELO

Madonna and Child, circa 1525
Black pencil, red pencil, white lead, and ink on paper,
21⅜ x 15⅝ inches
inv. 71F

This drawing, on a support made by gluing two sheets together, has often been called a "small cartoon." However, there is no evidence that this piece represents a preparatory phase of any work by Michelangelo or by artists connected to him. It is instead enlightening to think of this piece, without comparison in the corpus of Michelangelo's drawings, as a meditation—continually recurring in the artist's mind—on a maternity that is too painful for the mother to fully express her love for her son. It is no accident that the most notable *pentimento* on this page shows that Michelangelo had first drawn the Madonna's face in profile, with downcast eyes looking at the Child. Here and very often elsewhere, we find reminiscences of a tradition of maternal-filial tenderness that the artist was not able to accept from his predecessors, arriving instead at a dramatic absence of communication between mother and child. The image of the mother has a pose and an expression that are completely disconnected from the Child at her breast; her gaze is lost in the foreboding of future tragedy. In terms of the piece's content and psychology, the youthful Michelangelo had already dealt with the enigma of this gaze in his *Madonna of the Steps.* But over time the idea would evolve stylistically until it reached its highest expression in the mysterious *Madonna* of the New Sacristy in San Lorenzo, whose undeniable similarities to this drawing support the date we have accepted here.

Michelangelo, *Medici Madonna,* Florence, San Lorenzo, New Sacristy

A number of *pentimenti* can be seen in the Child as well. His head is traced with a delicate use of chiaroscuro that makes it similar to the Madonna's. His body, sketchy and finished with effects of painterly illusion, is completely void of holiness, as Paola Barocchi effectively summarizes when she speaks of "the putto's concrete plasticity."

The expressive disparity and technical rendering of the two figures make the general reading of the drawing problematic. This does not explain, however, why this disparity should be cited by several scholars of the stature of Berenson or Dussler to deny the attribution of the work to Michelangelo. Michelangelo the Younger had recognized the excellent quality of the "small cartoon," placing it in the Room of the Angels, that is in the (even spiritual) center of the seventeenth-century rooms that he had set up on the second floor of the Casa. The drawing's fame reached its apex during the nineteenth century, especially on the occasion of the four-hundredth anniversary of Michelangelo's birth in 1875, when the Casa Buonarroti's exhibition of drawings made the collection famous in Italy and abroad. In fact, an intervention discovered during a recent restoration probably dates from that time: the upper part of the page shows the signs of a cut, probably made for framing purposes but which, at the center, has removed part of the Madonna's veil.

BIBLIOGRAPHY

Paola Barocchi, *Michelangelo e la sua scuola. I disegni di Casa Buonarroti e degli Uffizi*, I, Florence 1962, pp. 149–152, no. 121.

Michael Hirst, *Michel-Ange dessinateur*, exhibition cat., Paris and Milan 1989, pp. 88–89, no. 36.

Flavio Fergonzi, in *Michelangelo nell'Ottocento. Rodin e Michelangelo*, edited by Maria Mimita Lamberti and Christopher Riopelle, exhibition cat., Casa Buonarroti, Milan 1996, pp. 166–169, no. 38.

8.

MICHELANGELO

Study for the Head of Leda, circa 1530
Red pencil on paper, 13⅝ x 10⅝ inches
inv. 7F

This drawing is unanimously recognized as one of the most beautiful and important of Michelangelo's graphic works. The bowed head, shown in profile, recalls the position of *Night* in the New Sacristy in San Lorenzo, and the splendid sureness of its vibrant line shows that it has been drawn from life. First Wilde, later followed by most scholars, supposed that the model was the artist's pupil Antonio Mini. One must keep in mind how often, in those times, male models posed for images of women. Yet it should be emphasized here how the sketch (lower left) of the details of the nose and eye, with long feminine eyelashes, softens the already delicate and thoughtful features of the profile.

It is widely agreed that this page refers to *Leda*, the lost painting whose history is interwoven with the complicated history of relations between Alfonso I d'Este, Duke of Ferrara, and Pope Julius II. In his alliance with Louis XII of France and his opposition to Venice, Alfonso had sided with forces opposed to the Pope and was excommunicated for it in the summer of 1510. Only two years later, after an unexpected defeat of the French forces in Italy, he opted to submit to the pontiff's power; he went to Rome, where he received a papal absolution. Three days after this event, on July 11, Julius II allowed him to go up on the scaffolding of the Sistine Chapel to see the ceiling, which at that point Michelangelo had almost entirely frescoed. The long dialogue with the duke, who was ecstatic in his admiration, ended with the

Attributed to Francesco Brina, *Leda and the Swan* (after Michelangelo), Florence, Casa Buonarroti, inv. Gallerie 1890, n. 5412

artist's promise to carry out a painting for him. Seventeen years later, while he was engaged in Florence's defense against Papal troops, Michelangelo went to Ferrara as Alfonso's guest in order to study the city's famous fortification system. At that time he let himself be persuaded to carry out Alfonso's longtime wish.

Perhaps it was the need to stay in hiding after the fall of Florence in August 1530 that gave Michelangelo time to work on the piece. Toward the middle of October of the same year, the "large hall painting" was finished, but it never reached Ferrara on account of the ignorance of the envoy sent by the Duke to pick up the painting: he referred to it, in front of the artist, as "not much." At this Michelangelo became irate and, as Condivi tells us, "having sent away the Duke's envoy, not long after he gave the painting to one of his apprentices." The apprentice was Antonio Mini, who appears to have been the recipient of not only the *Leda* but also several drawings and a preparatory cartoon of the painting. It has even been supposed, and not without reason, that the painting had been given to Mini by the artist not as a gift but so that he could sell it. In any case, it is known that Mini was in France between 1531 and 1532 and that the *Leda* was in his hands at that time. After his death in 1533, there are contradictory reports about disputes over the painting. According to Vasari, the painting wound up in François I's collections at Fontainebleau. Soon, however, all trace of it was lost; but Michelangelo's extraordinary vision, of which this drawing is the radiant prediction, has come down to us through numerous copies and derivations in the most varying techniques, among them the famous painting in the National Gallery in London, attributed to Rosso Fiorentino, as well as a small late sixteenth-century panel that is now exhibited in the Casa Buonarroti.

BIBLIOGRAPHY

Johannes Wilde, "Notes on the Genesis of Michelangelo's 'Leda,'" in *Fritz Saxl 1890–1948. A Volume of Memorial Essays from his Friends in England*, edited by D. J. Gordon, London 1957, pp. 270–280.
Michael Hirst, *Michel-Ange dessinateur*, exhibition cat., Paris and Milan 1989, pp. 92–93, no. 38.

9.

CRISTOFANO ALLORI (1577–1621)
    Portrait of Michelangelo Buonarroti the Younger, circa 1610
    Oil on canvas, 25⅝ x 17⅛ inches
    inv. 119

The first references to this fine portrait are found in the late-seventeenth-century inventory known as the Descrizione buonarrotiana, where it is recorded as being a work by Cristofano Allori, "and it is one of the good ones he made." There are no existing documents dealing with the commission, perhaps because of the close friendship, which, from at least 1608 on, directly tied Cristofano and Michelangelo the Younger. Further indication of the painter's privileged position among Buonarroti's artist friends is seen in *Michelangelo in Poetic Meditation,* a canvas

Giuliano Bugiardini, *Portrait of Michelangelo,*
Florence, Casa Buonarroti, inv. 65

painted by Zanobi Rosi in 1615 for the Gallery of the Casa Buonarroti, in which a portrait of Allori appears next to Michelangelo the Younger.

In the recent rearrangement of the seventeenth-century rooms on the Casa's upper story, Michelangelo the Younger's portrait has once again been hung in the position documented in the aforementioned Descrizione buonarrotiana—that is, alongside the painting portraying Michelangelo that has been attributed to Giuliano Bugiardini. It was Michelangelo the Younger himself who gave the two canvases identical frames, further demonstrating his desire to create a spiritual connection to his great ancestor.

These clues gleaned from anecdote and biography show the unlikelihood of Carlo Del Bravo's 1967 hypothesis that, for "stylistic reasons," the portrait of Michelangelo the Younger might be a copy carried out by Piermaria Baldi. Del Bravo cites Baldinucci's recollection that the Buonarroti heirs owned not only the Allori canvas but also "a beautiful copy of the same made in his youth by Piermaria Baldi, follower of Volterrano." In 1982 Claudio Pizzorusso took a stance similar to Del Bravo's, but in 1984 the work was accepted and shown as an original in the monographic exhibition on Cristofano Allori curated by Miles Chappell and held in the Sala delle Nicchie in Palazzo Pitti in Florence.

The Casa Buonarroti canvas served as the model for Vincenzo Franceschini's engraving, which was included in the 1746 edition of the *Life of Michelangelo Buonarroti* by Ascanio Condivi, edited by the antiquarian Francesco Gori.

BIBLIOGRAPHY

Carlo Del Bravo, "Su Cristofano Allori," in *Paragone* 205, 1967, p. 82, no. 14.

Claudio Pizzorusso, *Ricerche su Cristofano Allori*, Florence 1982, p. 13.

Miles Chappell, *Cristofano Allori*, exhibition cat., Florence 1984, p. 74, no. 22.

Pina Ragioneri, *Miguel Angel entre Florencia y Roma*, exhibition cat., Valencia 1997, p. 80, no. 10.

10.

MICHELANGELO BUONARROTI THE YOUNGER (1568–1647)
La Fiera e La Tancia, edited by Anton Maria Salvini, Florence, 1726
Typeset volume, bound, 13 x 9½ x 1⅞ inches
Biblioteca della Casa Buonarroti, B.1585ᵃ R.G.F.

The medallion on the rich frontispiece of this volume portrays, against a background view of Florence, the city personified as a crowned young woman, seated between the personification of the Arno River and the "Marzocco." A seated lion figure whose name means literally "small Mars," the Marzocco had become the symbol of Florence as a gesture of amends, after a flood of the Arno in 1333 carried off the statue of Mars, the protector of the pre-Christian city.

Michelangelo the Younger, organizer of culture, refined intellectual and collector, friend of artists and scholars, is featured here, through two of his works, primarily as a writer for the theater. *La Tancia*, a rustic comedy in verse, presented at the Medici court in 1611 and published anonymously the following year, is commonly considered his masterpiece. *La Fiera*, on the other hand, which debuted for the first time in the "Theatre of the Great Hall of the Uffizi" in 1619, was destined to become a lifetime project: revised and added to without end, it reached such enormous proportions that it took five days to present a total of twenty-five acts. The volume on display here contains the first typeset edition, annotated by the Florentine philologist Anton Maria Salvini (1653–1729).

BIBLIOGRAPHY

Maria Giovanna Masera, *Michelangelo Buonarroti il Giovane*, Turin 1941.

Claudio Varese, "Teatro, prosa, poesia," in *Il Seicento*, Milan 1967, pp. 543–549.

Michelangelo Buonarroti the Younger, *La Fiera. Redazione originaria (1619)*, edited by Umberto Limentani, Florence 1984.

LA FIERA
COMMEDIA
DI MICHELAGNOLO BUONARRUOTI
IL GIOVANE
E LA TANCIA
COMMEDIA RUSTICALE DEL MEDESIMO
COLL' ANNOTAZIONI
DELL' ABATE ANTON MARIA SALVINI
GENTILUOMO FIORENTINO

*E Lettor delle Lettere Greche nello Studio
Fiorentino.*

IN FIRENZE MDCCXXVI.

Nella Stamperia di S. A. R. Per li Tartini e Franchi.

Con Licenza de' Superiori.

TIBERIO TITI (1573–1627)

*The Placing of the Bust of Michelangelo on the Artist's Tomb
in the Church of Santa Croce, Florence, 1618–1620*
Oil on canvas, 14⅝ x 13⅝ inches
inv. G.A.A., n. 7486

This is the only known preliminary version of a work commissioned by Michelangelo Buonarroti the Younger for the four seventeenth-century rooms in the Casa Buonarroti.

Tiberio Titi received the commission in 1615, and documents show that the prepared canvas was taken to the artist's workshop on September 19 of that year. The first payment was made in August 1618, but the finished canvas was delivered only two years later, to be inserted in one of the precious ceiling panels of the Gallery, the first of the four rooms, where it can still be seen today.

Son of the painter and architect Santi di Tito, Tiberio Titi began his career in keeping with the customs of his time, as an apprentice in his father's workshop. He soon became his father's active collaborator, and his small paintings on copper were well known. In these works, which are lost to us today, the artist recounted "the most famous actions recorded in histories and fairy-tales." Even in painted works of larger dimensions, Titi often turned his hand to historical themes as well as to sacred subjects; he was such a renowned portraitist that he was in demand at the Medici court. Indeed he worked actively at court in the 1620s, until the arrival of Suttermans made Titi's style appear old-fashioned. One of his most well-known portraits is that of the newborn Leopoldo de' Medici (1617, now in Palazzo Pitti in Florence), the future cardinal whose famous collection included a large number of miniature portraits by Titi. Thus Michelangelo the Younger commissioned the canvas in question while the artist was still playing a role of great importance at court.

The canvas highlights the salient characteristics of Titi's style. One notices that the light illuminates the figures from the side, the light source being to the left and high up, strongly suggesting the influence of Caravaggio. Considering that the painting is located in the Gallery—the room where a singular biography of Michelangelo is told through pictures—the painting also reveals Titi's passion for history. And the

Tiberio Titi, *Construction of the Funerary Monument to Michelangelo in Santa Croce,* Florence, Casa Buonarroti, inv. 236

event recorded in his painting was a historical episode—the erection of a funeral monument to Michelangelo in the Church of Santa Croce—frozen here in the moment when the bust of the artist is raised on the tomb. Here we should keep in mind that Michelangelo died in his Roman residence of Macel de' Corvi on February 18, 1564. His nephew Leonardo didn't arrive until several days later, by which time his famous uncle had already been honored by a state funeral in the Church of the Santi Apostoli. So the sole heir had then to undertake the famous theft of the body, which he took

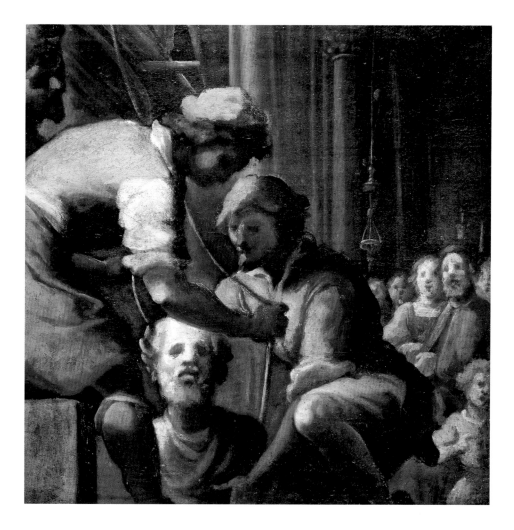

to Florence, as we learn from Vasari, disguised as "merchandise." There Michelangelo was honored by artists as well as the city in the church of San Lorenzo, before finding a definitive resting place in Santa Croce. The solemn funerary monument devoted to his memory was erected by Grand Duke Cosimo I de' Medici but carried out at Leonardo Buonarroti's expense. Thus in the present canvas we can clearly see Tiberio Titi's skill as a portraitist when he shows Leonardo with his wife Cassandra Ridolfi and two of their young children; one of these, Michelangelo the Younger, would grow up to be the commissioner of the art work but in the year of the scene being represented (1574), he was only six years old.

This oil sketch appears carefully executed and properly finished, further evidence of the attention with which the commissioner oversaw the setting up and decoration of the four Casa Buonarroti rooms. The family group portrayed had already been foreseen and is an indication of Michelangelo the Younger's filial piety. The changes that can be noted in the passage from the preliminary to the finished work are, in all probability, the result of precise "advice" given by the commissioner: for instance, the figure in the left foreground is, contrary to what had been suggested in the first version, bare to the waist and doesn't wear a cap; in this way, his curly hair and the muscles of his torso capture a brighter beam of light.

BIBLIOGRAPHY

Ugo Procacci, *La Casa Buonarroti a Firenze*, Milan 1965, p. 176.

Massimo Vezzosi, in *Arte in Toscana dal XV al XVIII secolo. Dipinti, disegni, sculture presentati da Massimo Vezzosi*, Florence 1995, pp. 40–42.

12.

ANDREA COMMODI (1560–1638)
Self-Portrait, circa 1625
Pastel on paper, 13¼ x 9¼ inches
inv. 91

The friendships that tied Michelangelo Buonarroti the Younger to the principal Florentine and Tuscan artists of his time find eloquent testimony in this self-portrait, which was given to the playwright by Andrea Commodi. This work of high quality, pervaded by a sense of concentrated melancholy, was mentioned with praise by Filippo Baldinucci in his *Notizie;* it is also the best-preserved and most complete of the numerous documented pastel works by Commodi.

The drawing was executed before 1626, the year that Michelangelo the Younger sent it to be inspected by an unspecified person, perhaps the very young Grand Duke Ferdinand II de' Medici; on that occasion he expressed his sincere appreciation of the piece. The pastel is an example from Commodi's late career, when the artist, after long stays in Rome and Cortona, had finally returned to Florence. The vertical and horizontal lines on the work (made more visible by a recent restoration) indicate that the sheet was originally intended to be used as a register. Again we see an instance of seventeenth-century frugality, as scarce paper was used and reused. The pastel technique employed by the artist makes the lines particularly evident. In the lower right, old handwriting reads: "And·ᵃ Commodi/fatto da Sé" (Andrea Commodi/by his own hand). Commodi's frequent visits to the Buonarroti household find further confirmation in a remarkable group of his own handwritten pages (conserved in the Uffizi Cabinet of Drawings and Prints), which contain copies of Michelangelo's drawings and models that were then in Michelangelo the Younger's possession.

BIBLIOGRAPHY

Gianni Papi, in *Il Seicento fiorentino. Arte a Firenze da Ferdinando I a Cosimo III. Disegno/Incisione/Scultura/ Art Minori,* exhibition cat., Florence 1986, p. 152, no. 2.97.

——————, *Andrea Commodi,* Florence 1994, p. 172, D 84.

And: Commodi
fatto da Se

13.

ATTRIBUTED TO ANASTAGIO FONTEBUONI (1571–1626)

Portrait of Three Young Members of the Buonarroti Family, circa 1620
Oil on canvas, 14⅝ x 19¾ inches
inv. 120

The first mention of this painting dates to 1857 and is found in a detailed description of the "Galleria Buonarroti" published by the erudite Agenore Gelli. An inventory taken two years later attributes the work to Cristofano Allori and identifies the figures represented as "the nephews of Michelangelo the poet." During the recent revival of studies on seventeenth-century Florence, the attribution was not deemed credible; thus a new proposal was put forward by Mina Gregori, who dates the work to the last period of Gregorio Pagani's activity—that is, to the first years of the seventeenth century. Gianni Papi, in various places, beginning in 1989, confidently attributes this agreeable little painting to Andrea Commodi and dates it around 1610. However, Luciano Berti's recent proposal seems convincing, for stylistic reasons, and is accepted here. The reference to Fontebuoni, once he had returned to his native city in 1620 after a long stay in Rome, means a later dating of the work; the relationship between Michelangelo the Younger and Fontebuoni and the latter's participation in the works for the Casa Buonarroti Gallery date from the early 1620s, when the artist began and completed the painting *Michelangelo Presents Himself to Julius II in Bologna.* However, these attempts at attributions and chronological placements are no help in identifying the three young men, traditionally thought to be Sigismondo, Michele, and Leonardo, Michelangelo the Younger's nephews.

Anastagio Fontebuoni, *Michelangelo Presents Himself to Julius II
in Bologna,* Florence, Casa Buonarroti, inv. 200

BIBLIOGRAPHY

Mina Gregori, "Una breve nota su Gregorio Pagani," in *Paragone* 353, 1979, p. 96, n. 7.
Gianni Papi, *Andrea Commodi,* Florence 1994, pp. 93–94, no. 23.

14.

The Discus Thrower's Arm (after Myron), first century AD
Marble, 22 x 10⅞ inches
inv. 18

The history of this precious artifact has recently been traced by Stefano Corsi, author of the complete catalogue of the Casa Buonarroti's Archaeological Collection. The first certain reference to the piece dates to the end of the seventeenth century when the work appears in the Descrizione buonarrotiana. The current placement of the work in the Room of Apollo is in keeping with the one mentioned in the Descrizione. In the second half of the nineteenth century, the *Arm*, under the heading of "Greek Sculpture," was exhibited in the same room where the *Madonna of the Steps* and the *Battle of the Centaurs* could be seen.

At the beginning of the twentieth century, Giulio Emanuele Rizzo recognized the Casa Buonarroti *Arm* as a fragment of a Roman copy of the *Discus Thrower*, a lost work by the great Greek sculptor Myron. This sculpture, one of the most famous of classical antiquity, carried out around the mid-fifth century BC, is known only through a series of copies. Myron had portrayed a young athlete in a crouch, preparing to throw the discus. The classical artist's great genius can be seen in his extraordinary ability to capture the split second of such rapid movement. According to Rizzo, the Florentine fragment could be compared to the copy of the *Discus Thrower* discovered in Castelporziano in 1906 and preserved today in the Roman National Museum. The scholar went so far as to carry out a three-dimensional reconstruction of his hypothesis, creating a plaster cast (visible today at the Museum of Plaster Casts at the University of Rome). Rizzo also hypothesized the provenance of the Buonarroti *Arm*, which he felt could be identified in the ancient marble arm described in the sixteenth century by Hieronymus Mercurialis as being part of the Medici collections housed in Palazzo Pitti in Florence.

Myron, *Discus Thrower* (Roman copy),
Rome, Roman National Museum

As for the date of the work, there is no certainty that it was made, as Rizzo maintained, in the age of Augustus. Recent studies have instead considered the possibility that this fragment of the *Discus Thrower* dates to Emperor Hadrian's time (second century AD). What is beyond dispute is the high quality of this Florentine piece, which had already been described in the late seventeenth century as "an ancient arm in marble, in the act of throwing a discus, and it is wonderfully made, showing even the muscles and veins."

BIBLIOGRAPHY

Stefano Corsi, *Casa Buonarroti. La collezione archaeologica*, Milan 1997, pp. 32–33.

15.

ANTONIO MONTAUTI, died 1743

Medal of Filippo Buonarroti, 1731
Bronze, 2½ inches in diameter
inv. 612

This medal is Antonio Montauti's last work as a medal maker. The artist, who lived between Florence and Rome, was also well known in his day as a sculptor.

On the verso, the medal shows the profile of Filippo Buonarroti, portrayed with a long curly wig and dressed as a senator. Around him appears the writing "QVEM NVLL(a) AEQVAVERIT AETAS," a motto that can be traced back to the Latin poet Silico Italico. On the same side, at the level of the bust's truncation, the artist has signed the work. On the recto, there are words at the center of a laurel wreath topped by a cameo of Minerva's head, reading "PHILIPPO BONARROTIO PATRICIO ET SENAT(ori) FLORENT(ino) FRANC(iscus) EQ(ues) VICTORIUS ANNO MDCCXXXI ROMAE D(edit) L(ibens) D(ono)." The writing is proof that the medal was commissioned (at his own expense) by Francesco Vettori, a member of the Etruscan Academy of Cortona. The medallion was cast in Rome by the medal maker Antonio Sarti, who used Montauti's model. An engraving of this work, done by Francesco Mazzoni, was inserted by Anton Francesco Gori in his edition of the *Life of Michelangelo* by Condivi, where he specified the meaning of Minerva's inclusion on the recto of the medal: "in Literature, or in deep Knowledge, our Senator Buonarroti . . . has not found, nor ever shall find, his equal."

Filippo Buonarroti (1661–1733) was a direct descendent of Michelangelo's family. He was the son of Leonardo, who was Michelangelo the Younger's nephew. Guided toward a career in law, Filippo was not yet twenty when he was sent to Rome, where he was able to deepen his knowledge of and passion for antiquity. Upon his return to Florence in 1699, by then famous and highly esteemed by his contemporaries, he lived for the rest of his life in the Via Ghibellina house, which he enriched with his collections of ancient art. He was buried in the Church of Santa Croce, near the tomb of his great ancestor.

BIBLIOGRAPHY

Benedetta Ballico, in *L'Accademia etrusca*, exhibition cat., Milan 1985, pp. 171–172, no. 161.

Daniela Gallo, *Filippo Buonarroti e la cultura antiquaria sotto gli ultimi Medici*, exhibition cat., Casa Buonarroti, Florence 1986, p. 48, no. 8.

Fiorenza Vannel and Giuseppe Toderi, *La medaglia barocca in Toscana*, Florence 1987, pp. 127–128, no. 106.

16.

ROBERT VAN AUDENAERD (1663–1743)
Gem with Portrait of Augustus (after a drawing by
Carlo Maratta, 1625–1713)
Engraving, 11¼ x 7⅞ inches
in Filippo Buonarroti, Osservazioni Istoriche sopra alcuni Medaglioni antichi
(Historical Observations about Some Ancient Medallions), Rome 1698, p. 45
Typeset volume, 11¼ x 8½ inches
Biblioteca della Casa Buonarroti, B.449.R.

This reproduction features the splendid Augustan gem that had been in the Roman collection of antiquities belonging to Cardinal Gaspare Carpegna, who was well known to Filippo Buonarroti. In 1785 the ancient cameo in chalcedony was mounted, by Louis Valadier, in a precious setting of marble, inlaid stones, gilded bronze, and enamel. In 1801 it became part of the collections at the Louvre, where it can still be seen today.

The name of the author of the drawing on which the engraving is based is Carlo Maratta, the most important Roman painter of the late seventeenth century, who was associated with an extensive production of engravings. During his youthful years of training, he gained experience in the techniques of etching and tried his hand at reproducing famous works of art; later, as his fame grew, his own paintings were the objects of engraved copies. In the case examined here, the commission for this engraving, given to an artist at the height of his career, can be explained by the cameo's value and fame. Maratta's appreciation of the piece can be inferred from the written preface to this volume by Filippo Buonarroti, who was a close friend of the artist.

Cameo depicting the bust of Augustus with setting
by Louis Valadier, Paris, Louvre

BIBLIOGRAPHY

Alvar Gonzáles-Palacios and François Baratte, Luigi Valadier au Louvre ou l'Antiquité exaltée, exhibition cat., Paris 1994, pp. 84–90.

Alessandro Angelini, in Arte e storia in biblioteca, edited by Stefano Corsi and Elena Lombardi, exhibition cat., Casa Buonarroti, Milan 1995, p. 31, no. 5.

AVGVSTVS

Ex jaſpide Chalcedonia bicolori

Apud Em. Card. Gaſp. de Carpinea.

Carol. Maratta del.   R.V. Auden. Ac. Sculp.

17.

Etruscan Cinerary Urn: Scene of Leave-taking in front of the Gate of Hades,
early first century BC
Polychrome terra-cotta
lid, 3⅛ x 10¼ x 6¾ inches; body, 7 x 8⅝ x 5⅜ inches
inv. 13

This urn, which is generically described as coming from Chiusi, is one of the Etruscan artifacts brought together in the Casa Buonarroti by antiquarian and scholar Filippo Buonarroti (see cat. 15). On the lid, the deceased is represented in a reclining position, completely covered by a mantle. The body of the urn shows a scene of leave-taking: in front of a closed doorway, two cloaked figures shake hands. Behind each man stands a female demon in a full-length gown, holding a torch. An inscription indicating the name of the deceased is written in red paint on the cornice. The small size and summary decoration of the urn suggest that it was to be used for a person of modest economic means. The presence of the Etruscan inscription dates the work to a period before 90 BC.

BIBLIOGRAPHY

Marisa Bonamici, in Daniela Gallo, *Filippo Buonarroti e la cultura antiquaria sotto gli ultimi Medici,* exhibition cat., Casa Buonarroti, Florence 1986, p. 74, no. 19.

Stefano Corsi, *Casa Buonarroti. La collezione archeologica,* Milan 1997, pp. 71–72.

5527

18.

Balsam Jar in the Shape of a Woman's Head (from central Italy),
third century BC
Bronze, 3¾ inches high
inv. 24

This piece probably came from a workshop that scholars have situated between Chiusi and Orvieto. Together with the cinerary urn (cat. 17), it entered the Buonarroti collections through Filippo Buonarroti, antiquarian and scholar. It is a balsam jar in the shape of a female head, with the hair set in locks and gathered together at the top of the figure's head. In the top knot there is a circular aperture that must have been covered with a lid, now lost.

The balsam jar is one of a variety of luxury goods that were based to some extent on rare Greek models but were Etruscan in form and use, which was twofold: the jar served both for female beautification as well as for burial treasures. The small bronze is placed on a base of inlaid marble that probably dates from the time of Filippo Buonarroti.

BIBLIOGRAPHY

Marisa Bonamici, in Daniela Gallo, *Filippo Buonarroti e la cultura antiquaria sotto gli ultimi Medici*, exhibition cat., Casa Buonarroti, Florence 1986, pp. 79–80, no. 31.

Les Etrusques et l'Europe, exhibition cat., Paris and Milan 1992, p. 382, no. 384.

Stefano Corsi, *Casa Buonarroti. La collezione archeologica*, Milan 1997, pp. 50–51.

Piazza San Lorenzo at the end of the nineteenth century

MICHELANGELO AND THE SAN LORENZO COMPLEX IN FLORENCE

Despite the press of market stalls, anyone approaching Piazza San Lorenzo in Florence from the direction of Palazzo Medici Riccardi is immediately struck by the imposing architectural complex of San Lorenzo. Michelangelo's involvement with this structure distinguishes his architectural activity in Florence and makes for a story in which official relationships are established and severed, friends are sometimes betrayed, and lengthy interruptions enable him to quarry marble in Pietrasanta and Seravezza. But above all, it is the story of an aesthetic tension that was destined to result in either unrealized projects or supreme masterpieces. This protracted episode occupied the artist constantly from 1516 until 1534, the year in which he finally left for Rome, never to return.

In March 1513, Giovanni de' Medici (1475–1521), the son of Lorenzo the Magnificent (1449–1492), was elected Pope and assumed the name of Leo X. Two and a half years later, between November and December 1515, he decided to return to his native city on a formal visit. Florence greeted him with pomp and splendor that involved the erection of many temporary constructions, including a number of triumphal arches and an impressive structure—commissioned from Jacopo Sansovino (1486–1570) and Andrea del Sarto (1486–1530)—to mask the rough façade of the Cathedral of Santa Maria del Fiore. This covering is said to have caught the pontiff's imagination, giving him the idea to set up a competition for designs for the San Lorenzo façade. The Medici had been patrons of the incomplete basilica, designed by Brunelleschi, since its foundation in 1421 and had designated it as their family burial place.

Michelangelo deeply admired the genius of Filippo Brunelleschi (1377–1446), and doubtless he was attracted by the possibility of adding to the work created by the man responsible for the cathedral's dome. Leo X's proposal also came at a time when the artist seemed to be devoting particular attention to problems of architectural composition. With regard to this point, Johannes Wilde has recalled the monumental structure of the 1516 project for the tomb of Julius II, Pope from 1503 to 1513. From the same period (1515–1517), there are also the drawings copying particular details from ancient architecture taken from a contemporary document, the so-called *Coner Codex,* and there also seems to be clear reference to the grandiose spatial scansions of the Sistine Chapel ceiling, which had been completed four years before the beginning of the whole Laurentian saga.

Michelangelo, *Studies of Ancient Architecture*, Florence, Casa Buonarroti, inv. 1A verso

These projects are often called to account for the architectural "turning point" of 1516. They also serve to remind us that no Michelangelo scholars have ever found a way to precisely trace the complex genesis of the turning point's first important step, namely the project for the façade of San Lorenzo; nor has it ever been discovered why such a fully developed and tormented project was never carried out. On this subject, Vasari—in his *Lives* of Jacopo Sansovino, Michelangelo, and Leonardo da Vinci— contradicts himself several times, while Condivi avoids, as always, tainting the shining pedestal on which he has placed his idol. What is factually certain is that, besides Michelangelo, the protagonists of the project were initially Antonio (1483–1536) and Giuliano da Sangallo (1445–1516), Jacopo Sansovino, and Raphael (1483–1520), while Baccio d'Agnolo (1462–1543) modestly maintained his secondary role as long as he was in a position to do so.

In any case, it seems reasonable to hypothesize that, at the outset, Michelangelo was given only the task of supervising the sculptural decoration, while Jacopo Sansovino had Baccio d'Agnolo make a wooden model for the façade, a work that was much appreciated at the time but has since been lost. Over the year 1516, the contest for such a prestigious commission led to the formation of rival camps: on one side artists such as Antonio and Giuliano da Sangallo, Raphael, and Sansovino, and on the other Michelangelo, who astutely formed a collaborative pact with Baccio d'Agnolo, the least dangerous of his competitors; indeed, the master did not find it difficult to get rid of him subsequently.

There followed a series of complicated maneuvers on Michelangelo's part, documented by the correspondence dating from those months of Domenico Buoninsegni, secretary to the Pope. Finally, in the autumn of 1516, Michelangelo obtained from Leo X the commission for the architectural design of the façade. In December of the same year, he went to Rome to present a preliminary design, which was duly approved. In the early months of 1517, Baccio produced a wooden model based on that design, but Michelangelo declared that his ideas had been totally misunderstood and, in a letter dated March 20, he defined it as "a child's thing." On

Michelangelo, *"Second Project" for the Façade of San Lorenzo,* Florence,
Casa Buonarroti, inv. 47A

March 27 he was given total responsibility for the work, and Baccio was removed from the project on the grounds—probably unfounded and certainly proudly denied by the artist—of improper and hypocritical behavior.

In his letter to Buoninsegni dated May 2, a famous missive among the many he sent in those months to the Pope's secretary, Michelangelo commented on the new clay model that he had prepared in the meantime. He asked for trust, freedom, and money, because his "soul was sufficient to make of this work for the façade of San Lorenzo, both architecturally and sculpturally, the glory of all Italy." In June, Sansovino was also removed from the project; he did not depart, however, without uttering and writing some extremely invective comments.

After these somewhat dishonorable preliminaries—a further demonstration, nonetheless, of his forceful power and need for solitude—Michelangelo finally managed to get free of his competitors. He proceeded to produce an exceptional solution to a problem that constantly assailed Renaissance architects when they had to correctly apply classical orders to the irregular façades of churches with a basilical plan. Michelangelo dealt with the issue by making the viewer forget the external structure of the church by hiding it behind the secular front of a splendid private palace.

The general design of the façade went through three main phases, all documented in three drawings from the Casa Buonarroti Collection. The first phase, still uncertain but full of daring, can be seen in the project presented to the Pope in December 1516 and probably illustrated in the large sheet inv. 45A ("first project"; see cat. 19). A month or so later, Michelangelo developed the concept expressed in drawing 47A ("second project"). In the spring of 1517, he arrived at the clearly delineated image visible in sheet 43A ("third project"). The last was, in all likelihood, translated into the famous large wooden model currently displayed in the Casa Buonarroti Museum. This model was completed toward the end of the year, after the artist's long illness, which held up the work; it reflects quite faithfully the passage from the initial

Michelangelo, *"Third Project" for the Façade of San Lorenzo*, Florence, Casa Buonarroti, inv. 43A

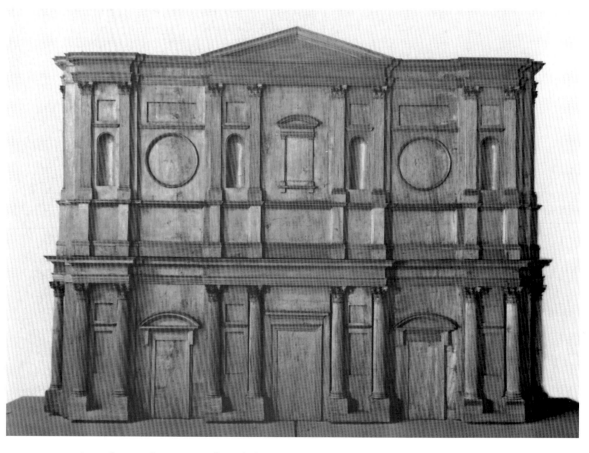

According to the project of Michelangelo, *Model for the Façade of San Lorenzo*, Florence, Casa Buonarroti, inv. 518

design to the realization, as established in a contract stipulated between Pope Leo X and Michelangelo on January 19, 1518.

In the following two years, 1518 and 1519, the artist spent most of his time extracting marble from the quarries in Pietrasanta and Seravezza. On March 10, 1520, he took note of the rescision of the contract (even if it only concerned the supply of marble), and the material gathered until then was used for the floor of Santa Maria del Fiore. But the construction work certainly continued, albeit slowly, until April 1521, the year of Leo X's death. After the brief pontificate of his successor, Adrian VI, Clement VII became Pope in November 1523. He, too, was a member of the Medici family, and, as Vasari records, he stated more than once his intention to resume work on the façade. It was not until his death in 1534 that all hope of realizing this large-scale and tormented project definitively faded.

Clement VII's interest in the basilica of San Lorenzo can also be seen from the fact that in 1525 he entrusted Michelangelo with the task of creating, for the church choir, a ciborium where reliquaries could be displayed. Michelangelo accepted the commission, but not the location suggested by Clement VII. In fact, after lengthy correspondence with the papal administrator Giovanfrancesco Fattucci, he decided to construct a reliquary tribune on the inside of the church façade above the central portal. The work was carried out between 1531 and July 1533, when it received the Pope's praises.

※

Though pained and angered by years of vain effort and hard work, beginning in September 1519 Michelangelo turned his attention to another job, also commissioned by Leo X. The Pope's nephew Lorenzo, Duke of Urbino, had died in May of that

Michelangelo, *Resurrected Christ*, Rome, Santa Maria sopra Minerva

year, and three years earlier, his brother Giuliano, Duke of Nemours, had also died. This double bereavement undoubtedly drew Leo X's attention away from the façade, a celebration of the power of the living, and toward the realization of a new family chapel. Located at the end of the transept of the basilica of San Lorenzo, it was to offer an appropriately decorous setting for the tombs of the most recent generations of the Medici family. Widely known today as the New Sacristy and considered one of the high points of Michelangelo's almost superhuman artistic career, this second chapel was intended by Leo X to be a replica of the Old Sacristy, the imposing sepulchral monument of the family's ancestors designed by Brunelleschi and situated at the opposite end of the transept.

However, the new task coincided with an extremely difficult period in the artist's life. The lengthy and highly complex task of building the tomb of Julius II in Rome was still unfinished, even though Michelangelo had already carried out a number of the statues for it, including his *Moses.* The *Resurrected Christ* produced for the

Michelangelo, Reliquary Tribune, Florence, San Lorenzo

church of Santa Maria sopra Minerva in Rome and the windows of the Palazzo Medici in Florence certainly could not compensate for the bitterness caused by the many obstacles that had effectively halted construction work on the San Lorenzo façade. It can reasonably be supposed that Michelangelo's extraordinary devotion to the new work, its admirable development, and its innovative results all originated from his will to react to an uncertain and frustrated state of mind.

The Medici Chapel commission came at the same time as the proposal to design—also inside the convent of San Lorenzo—a library to preserve the extensive and valuable collection of volumes begun by Cosimo il Vecchio de' Medici (1389–1462) and considerably enlarged by Lorenzo the Magnificent. But Michelangelo chose to concentrate first of all on the new mausoleum, a choice that appears by no means accidental. The chapel was intended to house the tombs of Lorenzo the Magnificent and his brother Giuliano, as well as Giuliano, Duke of Nemours, and Lorenzo, Duke of Urbino.

A good deal of information about the time it took and the way in which the work was conducted can be gleaned from a document discovered by Gino Corti and published in 1964 by Alessandro Parronchi: the *ricordanza* (memoirs) of Giovan Battista Figiovanni, administrator of the Laurentian complex during that period. This important document establishes the starting date of the work as November 4, 1519,

Michelangelo, New Sacristy (exterior), Florence

with the destruction of a number of houses recently purchased by the Medici. Part of the external wall of the church was also torn down in order to clear the necessary space for the new chapel. Moreover, the memoir seems to show that Michelangelo did not work from existing designs or buildings but rather constructed the edifice from its foundations. Despite the strong position assumed by Wilde and the numerous subsequent proposals by scholars such as Caroline Elam and Howard Burns, who also supported this view, critics are still divided on these opposing hypotheses. Nonetheless, there is no doubting the importance of Michelangelo's role in designing the chapel.

The project kept Michelangelo busy for approximately fifteen years, a period that was also decisive for the consolidation of his identity as an architect and sculptor. In the New Sacristy, we can clearly see highlighted—through an increasingly complex development—the moment of passage from the classically decorative language of the San Lorenzo façade to the successful balance of architectural and sculptural elements that is characteristic of the Laurentian Library. In fact, the New

Michelangelo, Tomb of Lorenzo de' Medici, Duke of Urbino,
Florence, New Sacristy

Michelangelo, *River God*, Florence, Casa Buonarroti, inv. Gallerie 1890, n. 1802

Michelangelo, Tomb of Giuliano de' Medici, Duke of Nemours,
Florence, New Sacristy

Sacristy's distinctive appeal lies in its dramatic, restless, and precarious equilibrium
between architecture and sculpture.

Michelangelo intended for the interior of the chapel to have an imposing set of
sculptures, but these were only executed in part. For example, four reclining male
figures, to be positioned on the floor, were never realized; these were meant to per-
sonify the *River Gods,* in keeping with ancient iconography in use since Hellenistic
times. A model of one of these large figures, made by Michelangelo himself, is preserved in the Casa Buonarroti. A smaller sketch model (see cat. 23) is included in this
exhibition. The works that were completed and finally carved in marble reveal an intense graphic study and an abiding interest in ancient statuary.

As we have seen, work on the chapel statues as well as the complex decoration
of the walls and dome—carried out in marble and stucco—continued for many
years, up until Michelangelo's final departure for Rome. It was an enormous task, and
in spite of his inclinations he had to take on quite a number of assistants, not only
stonemasons but also sculptors such as Silvio Cosini (1497–circa 1547), Raffaello da

Michelangelo, New Sacristy (interior), Florence

Montelupo (circa 1505–1576), Giovannangelo Montorsoli (1507–1563), and even Giovanni da Udine, the great specialist in stucco work.

At the time of Michelangelo's departure for Rome in 1534, the completed works included the full figures of the two dukes, the personifications of the four times of day (*Day, Night, Dawn, Dusk*), and the *Madonna and Child, Saint Cosmas,* and *Saint Damian,* which were all three destined for the chapel altar. Of these works, only the last two were not personally carried out by Michelangelo, having been executed according to his design by Montorsoli and Raffaello da Montelupo. All these works were left abandoned for years on the floor of the chapel and in the artist's studio in Via Mozza, for the death of the second Medici Pope led to the interruption of yet another Medici-sponsored undertaking.

The chapel was opened around 1545 with the personifications of the four times of day already in position, but it was not until 1559 that the *Madonna* and two saints were positioned on the large tomb, which, from that year on, would contain the bodies of Lorenzo the Magnificent and his brother Giuliano. In 1563 the Florentine Accademia del Disegno proposed to Duke Cosimo I, through Vasari, to complete the decoration of the chapel with statues and paintings to be carried out by a number of masters ranging from Benvenuto Cellini (1500–1571) to Agnolo Bronzino (1503–1572). Fortunately, the proposal was not accepted, possibly due, as Paola Barocchi has suggested, to the tacit dissent of Michelangelo.

Today's visitor to the New Sacristy finds no trace of this long and tortuous story, which witnessed the creation of some supreme masterpieces but left other projects at the planning stage or only partially completed. Rather, the visitor is only aware of *pietra serena* and marble being united here in a show of absolute perfection.

Michelangelo, Reading Room of the Medici Laurentian Library, Florence

The construction of the Laurentian Library, which was commissioned in 1519 but not started immediately because Michelangelo was occupied with the New Sacristy, only got under way in 1524, partly as a result of the election of Pope Clement VII. Having resolved the problem of where to locate it within the Laurentian complex, the new edifice, the foundations, the external buttresses, and the structure of the reading room were built between 1524 and 1525. In April, Clement VII made a written request to the artist to design a "secret library in which to keep certain books more precious than the others"; this was to replace the previously envisaged chapel at one end of the reading room. This small library did not, however, get beyond the design stage (see cats. 24–25). In the autumn, Michelangelo declared that he was ready to construct the vestibule even though the problem of illumination had not been entirely resolved. The work proceeded rapidly, but in the summer and autumn of 1526 the Pope ran into financial difficulties, and Michelangelo was asked to limit costs. These economic problems were compounded the following year by a much more calamitous event, the sacking of Rome by the troops of Emperor Charles V.

Between 1525 and 1530, Florence experienced its brief and heroic life as a republic, of which Michelangelo was a fervent supporter. (See his designs for the fortifications of the city, cat. 30.) The work on San Lorenzo effectively remained at a standstill until the return of the Medici in 1530. But building had come to a halt when the reading room was largely finished, with the exception of the ceiling, the floor, and the wooden furnishing: the characteristic two-color traditional Florentine style (*pietra serena* and white plaster) had not yet been bathed in the bright color of the linden and pine wood of the reading benches and the ceiling, which would later

Michelangelo, Vestibule of the Medici Laurentian Library, Florence

be mirrored in the red and white terra-cotta of the floor (see cats. 28–29). Michelangelo handed over the job of producing the benches—which since 1524 had been considered an integral element of the room's architecture—to woodcarvers in 1533. From the memoirs of Figiovanni we learn that in September 1534, shortly before the death of Pope Clement VII, six carpenters were at work on the benches and six on the ceiling, the design of which had already been completed in 1526. The floor, a wonderful mirror of the ceiling, was executed much later, between 1549 and 1554, from a design by Nicolò Tribolo (1500–1550).

From the numerous drawings (almost certainly by Michelangelo himself) of Michelangelo's design for the vestibule and the celebrated entrance stairs, we can deduce the strength of his imprint on the completed work. The realization of the vestibule and the stairs was an extremely complicated process. As Alessandro Nova so succinctly puts it, the work went on "for more than thirty years during which there were two patrons (Clement VII and Cosimo I dei Medici), Michelangelo moved definitively to Rome and other non-authorized artists (such as Tribolo) or authorized ones (like Ammannati and Vasari) continued what had been left undone by the master." From Rome, Michelangelo responded neither to his patrons nor to the artists requesting instructions on how to proceed with this part of the building. He limited himself to sending, in January 1559, a small clay model of the stairs, proposing that they "be made of wood," establishing a clear link with the wooden furnishings of the reading room. But Cosimo I opted for a longer-lasting material and ordered Bartolomeo Ammannati (1511–1592) to use stone. The library was opened to the public in June 1571. At the beginning of the twentieth century, an "arbitrary and mediocre finishing restoration" (Bruno Contardi) was carried out, limited to the vestibule ceiling and the exterior of the space.

19.

MICHELANGELO

First Design for the Façade of San Lorenzo, 1516
Pen, watercolor, and charcoal on paper, 28½ x 34¼ inches
inv. 45A

At the end of the seventeenth century, this piece was one of a limited number of Michelangelo's drawings deemed fit to be hung on the walls of the monumental rooms located on the main floor of the Via Ghibellina building. Almost all the other drawings were kept bound in volumes and stored inside cabinets. There have been various discussions in the last century as to whether this drawing was done by the artist himself. Well-founded arguments supporting this view have been produced in recent years, particularly as a result of research by Michael Hirst and Henry A. Millon. The work is distinctive among those owned by the Casa Buonarroti for its technical peculiarities as well as for its size, which makes it the largest drawing in the Collection. In fact, it consists of six sheets joined by a kind of support on the back. Different techniques of representation can be seen: in the lower part, straight ink lines for the architectural forms and pale watercolors for the figures, while in the upper part dark watercolors predominate. The recent studies also support the hypothesis that the drawing dates from the end of 1516, thus relating it to the early phases of Michelangelo's design for the façade of the San Lorenzo basilica (see p. 81).

The subjects of the two reliefs above the door on the left-hand side of the sheet can be clearly seen: above, Saint Lawrence before the Emperor Decius, and below, the martyrdom of the saint. The antique manner that characterizes all the other rapidly sketched figures, including those on the attic, is not enough to allow iconographic identification.

BIBLIOGRAPHY

Michael Hirst, "Addenda Sansoviniana," in *The Burlington Magazine* CXIV, 1972, p. 165, n. 10.

Henry A. Millon, in Henry A. Millon and Vittorio Magnago Lampugnani, *Rinascimento da Brunelleschi a Michelangelo. La rappresentazione dell'architettura*, exhibition cat., Milan 1994, pp. 566–567, no. 224.

20.

MICHELANGELO

Sketches of Marble Blocks with Notes in the Artist's Handwriting, 1517
Pen and red pencil on paper, 12⅜ x 8⅝ inches
Archivio Buonarroti, L, 82

The Archivio Buonarroti conserves a great number of pages such as these, which must have belonged to Michelangelo's notebooks and are related to his various works. The documentary value of these papers has frequently been recognized. They demonstrate Michelangelo's habit of making rapid sketches accompanied by very precise indications of measurement for the stonemasons, who then had to work out the size and shape of the blocks of marble the artist planned to use.

The drawing on display here, which is also remarkable for its handwritten notes, was part of a notebook of thirty pages. Nineteen of these, including this sheet, show the outlines of blocks of marble delivered to Michelangelo by quarrymen with whom he had stipulated contracts in 1516–1517 and whom the artist indicates on each page. In this case, the quarrymen are named, on the recto and verso, by just their initials (B for Bello, Ch for Cagione, L for Leone, M for Mancino). The letters are inserted in the artist's own mark, formed by three interwoven circles symbolizing the three arts. The presence of Mancino (that is, Bartolomeo di Giampaolo di Cagione da Torano) provides this group of drawings with a chronological point of reference, because the quarryman was already dead by October 23, 1518. This is proven by a document in the Opera del Duomo in Florence that has been opportunely brought to light by Lucilla Bardeschi Ciulich. As a result, these drawings, despite the common claims of Michelangelo criticism, cannot be considered pertinent to the work on the New Sacristy, because the first contracts for the building date to April 1521. Bardeschi Ciulich rightly connects these pages to the "book" with drawings of blocks of marble mentioned on more than one occasion in a contract stipulated in Carrara on August 18, 1517, by the notary Ser Galvano Parlontiotto di Ser Nicola. The initials of Ser Galvano recur frequently in this "book" and can also be seen on the verso of the drawing on exhibit.

The interest generated by this document's exact recording should not overshadow its aesthetic value and the strength of the strokes that, as Paola Barocchi points out, "suddenly go beyond contingency, proudly providing a glimpse of the creation."

BIBLIOGRAPHY

Paola Barocchi, *Michelangelo e la sua scuola. I disegni dell'Archivio Buonarroti*, Florence 1964, pp. 72–73, n. 324.

Lucilla Bardeschi Ciulich, "I marmi di Michelangelo," in Marco Dezzi Bardeschi, *La difficile eredità. Architettura a Firenze dalla Repubblica all'assedio*, exhibition cat., Florence 1994, pp. 100–105.

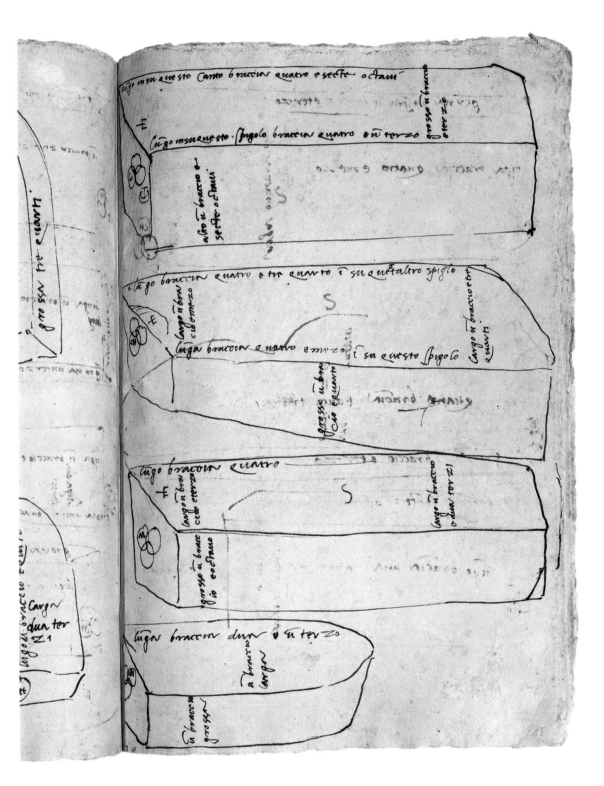

21.

MICHELANGELO

Profile of the Base of a Column for the New Sacristy, circa 1520–1525
Pen on paper, 12¾ x 5¾ inches
inv. 59A

As Michelangelo's handwritten note indicates—"*modano* [template or model]
for the columns of the sacristy's double tomb"—the drawing is a design for
the bases of columns for the double tomb (never carried out) of Lorenzo
the Magnificent and his brother Giuliano. Michelangelo was commissioned, before
July 21, 1524, to make the work. *Modano* is an old technical term for the natural-size
profile of an architectural element that serves to guide the masons' work. In the period just before his final departure for Rome in 1534, Michelangelo gave papers of this
kind, indicating the precise tasks that were to be carried out in his absence, to
Giovannangelo Montorsoli, who in 1533 had been charged with the responsibility for
carrying out the double tomb.

BIBLIOGRAPHY

Tracy Cooper, in Henry A. Millon and Vittorio Magnago Lampugnani, *Rinascimento da Brunelleschi
a Michelangelo. La rappresentazione dell'architettura,* exhibition cat., Milan 1994, pp. 497–498, n. 114.

il modano della colonna della se questura doppia di sagrestia

22

MICHELANGELO

Pilaster Base for the New Sacristy, with the Artist's Handwriting, 1524
Red pencil and pen on paper, 11⅛ x 8½ inches
inv. 10A

The nephew of Pope Leo X, Lorenzo de' Medici, Duke of Urbino, died in May 1519, while his brother Giuliano de' Medici, Duke of Nemours, had died three years previously. The double bereavement convinced the pontiff, who was very attached to his Medici ancestry (he was the son of Lorenzo the Magnificent), to create a new family chapel to be located at the end of the transept of the San Lorenzo basilica. In fact, for lack of space, the dead members of the most recent generations of the Medici family could not be buried in the Old Sacristy at the opposite end of the transept; there an imposing sepulchral monument for the family ancestors had been designed and executed by Filippo Brunelleschi, with sculptural work by Donatello, between 1422 and 1428. Apart from housing the tombs of the two dukes, the new construction was also intended to contain the tombs of Lorenzo the Magnificent and his brother Giuliano.

This second chapel, which is now known throughout the world as the New Sacristy and is considered one of the high points of Michelangelo's superhuman career, was intended by the papal patron to be nothing more than a replica of Brunelleschi's sacristy. However, the task of realizing the work was entrusted to Michelangelo at a particularly dramatic period of his life. The lengthy and highly complex task of building the tomb of Julius II in Rome was still unresolved (prompting Michelangelo to refer to it as "the tragedy of the tomb"); work on the façade of the San Lorenzo basilica (also commissioned by Leo X), to which he had passionately dedicated himself for more than three years, was effectively interrupted by the imposed need to design another work. Michelangelo began work on the new project with Leo X and then, from 1524 onward, with his successor Clement VII, who was also a member of the Medici family.

We recall this historical information as a prologue for understanding this very suggestive document, full of profound references: here the power of architectural invention, the fascination of the master's handwriting, as well as the mysterious and emotional meaning of the words come together to form an eloquent synthesis of the complex human and artistic reasons that gave birth to the New Sacristy. On the one hand, we can't help but notice—even without wanting to emphasize it unduly—the anthropomorphic interpretation that transforms the profile of the base (lower right) into a human profile. While it is not clear whether it is a caricature, the face is undoubtedly crying out. On the other hand, the text suggests, beyond the neo-Platonic contrivances raised by a number of academics, the essential themes of Time and Death:

> the sky and the earth, the day and the night, speak and say: with our rapid course we have led Duke Giuliano to his death; it is more than right that he should take his vengeance as he does, and his vengeance is this, that as we have killed him, he, in dying, has taken away our light and with his closed eyes has barred shut ours, which no longer shine above the earth. What, then, would he have done with us had he lived?

el cielo

e la terra

e fflli elamete parlon odichono noi abiano cholnostro veloce chorso cho de
cto allamorte olducha guliano e bo gusto che eno facci vedecta chome fa
el aveduocta e questa che muodo inoi morto lui lui chosi r e e ortolta la
luce amoi e choglio chi chiusi a servato enostri ch no rispledo piu so
pra laterra che arrebbe dinoi duch fasto morte in vea

j cesto dctocta secha

casto ottota fecta

The drawing appears to have been cut out; in fact, it was originally part of a folio that is also in the Buonarroti Collection (inv. 9A), in which bases of pilasters for the New Sacristy are depicted in a similar way. The connection between these two splendid studies and the bases of the double pilasters for the dukes' tombs was first made by Popp and has since been almost unanimously accepted by scholars. The written text *el cielo e la terra* on the top margin is by Michelangelo himself and is repeated underneath in a later handwriting, which some experts (including Barocchi) have identified as the hand of the artist's great-nephew Michelangelo Buonarroti the Younger. The note probably alludes to the artist's intention to place two allegorical figures portraying the sky and the earth in two niches, one on each side of the statue of Giuliano. This is just one of Michelangelo's many ideas for the interior of the New Sacristy that would never be developed beyond the initial design stage.

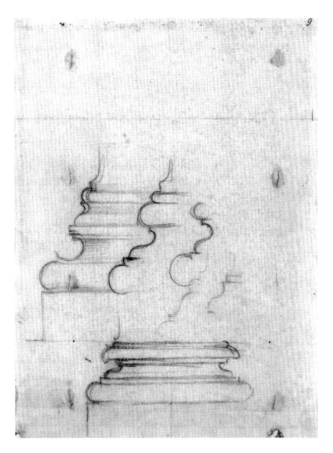

Michelangelo, *Base of a Pilaster for the New Sacristy*, Florence, Casa Buonarroti, inv. 9A

BIBLIOGRAPHY

Anny E. Popp, *Die Medici-Kapelle Michelangelos*, Munich 1922, p. 129, no. 12.

Paola Barocchi, *Michelangelo e la sua scuola. I disegni di Casa Buonarroti e degli Uffizi*, 2 vols., Florence 1962, I, pp. 85–86, nos. 61, 62.

Charles de Tolnay, *Corpus dei disegni di Michelangelo*, 4 vols., Novara 1975–1980, II, pp. 37–38, no. 201.

Giulio Carlo Argan and Bruno Contardi, *Michelangelo architetto*, Milan 1990, p. 181.

23.

ATTRIBUTED TO MICHELANGELO

River God, circa 1525
Tallow, pitch, and wax turpentine, 8¾ inches long
inv. 542

The model, as it is seen today, is made up of several fragments (the two thighs, an arm, and the torso), which between 1920 and 1928, as Wilde has shown, were put back together to form a single figure. In the 1859 Casa Buonarroti inventory we find the earliest mention of these pieces, while the attribution to Michelangelo was put forth by Fabbrichesi, the first curator of the Casa Buonarroti, in his 1865 guide. Today the master's authorship of the work is generally agreed upon, although there are still some doubts on the part of several scholars. For instance, in 1990 Jean Gaborit dated the model to the years 1520–1521, attributing it to an artist close to Michelangelo.

Even the identification of the work's subject has not been entirely agreed upon. Thode referred to it briefly in 1913 as "a study for a crucified thief," and considered the work "probably authentic." Wilde, although he attributed the piece to Michelangelo, interpreted it in 1928 as a study for one of the *Prisoners* for the tomb of Julius II; it is on his authority (shared by, among others, Hartt 1968 and 1987, and by Wittkower 1977) that perhaps we owe the fact that in 1969 the model was still displayed in an upright position, as is shown in a photo by Alinari of the same year. In 1954, de Tolnay, making reference to Wilde, declared that the model could be seen as a figure both vertically and horizontally. In 1970, however, he expressed his conviction that the model's position could only have been "reclining," and he connected the work to the four river gods that Michelangelo designed to place on the floor of the New Sacristy. This conviction must have been the tradition in Casa Buonarroti: when the Casa's collection of models was reorganized in 1920, care was taken to arrange the torso (that is, the most visible fragment) in a reclining position and turned on its right side, in keeping with the supposition put forth by Wilde that this work represents a river god. The horizontal arrangement of the work, as it is seen today, was made in the 1970s, and it presents remarkable similarities to the exciting model of a river god, of large dimensions and undisputed attribution, that is currently displayed in the Museum of the Casa Buonarroti.

BIBLIOGRAPHY

Johannes Wilde, "Due bozzetti di Michelangelo ricomposti," in *Dedalo*, VIII, 1928, pp. 666–670.

———, "Zwei Modelle Michelangelos für das Julius-Grabmal," in *Jahrbuch der Kunsthistorischen Sammlungen in Wien*, N.F., II, 1928, pp. 208–212.

Charles de Tolnay, *Michelangelo*, IV, Princeton 1954, p. 157, no. 1.

Flavio Fergonzi, in *Michelangelo nell'Ottocento. Rodin e Michelangelo*, edited by Maria Mimita Lamberti and Christopher Riopelle, exhibition cat., Casa Buonarroti, Milan 1996, pp. 162–165, no. 37.

24

MICHELANGELO

Project for the Small Library in the Laurentian Library, circa 1525
Pen on paper, 11⅛ x 16¼ inches
inv. 79A

The "Small Library," commissioned from Michelangelo by the Medici Pope
Clement VII in 1525, was designed to house the collection's most precious
books. In the artist's design, it should have occupied the space previously set
aside for the chapel, where the reading room of the Laurentian Library was supposed
to end. But this setting, conceived as a sort of parallel space to the Library's entrance
atrium, was never carried out. In these two drawings we can follow the development
of Michelangelo's design, characterized by the gradual definition of the articulated
forms of the walls by means of columns, niches, and pilasters. Some of the handwritten notes on drawing 80A help to present his ideas about the illumination of the
Small Library, while others refer to instructions for buying a house, instructions given
by the Pope and transcribed by the artist.

25.

MICHELANGELO

Plan of the Small Library in the Laurentian Library (with Writings in the Artist's Hand), 1525
Pen and brown watercolors on paper, 8⅜ x 11 inches
inv. 80A

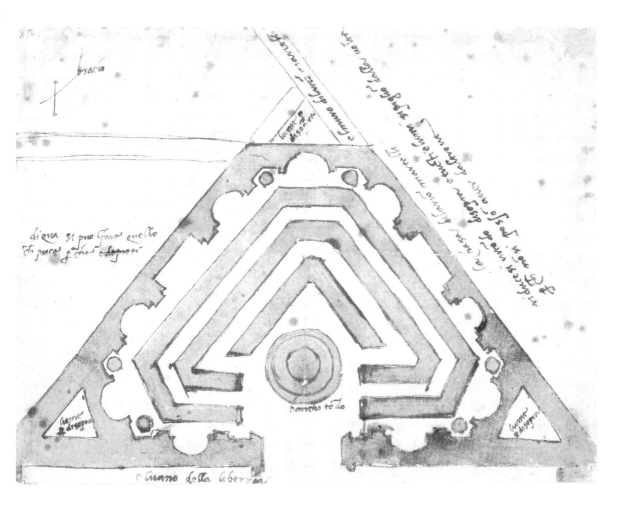

BIBLIOGRAPHY

Paola Barocchi, *Michelangelo e la sua scuola. I disegni di Casa Buonarroti e degli Uffizi*, Florence 1962, pp. 111–112, no. 88.

Giulio Carlo Argan and Bruno Contardi, *Michelangelo architetto*, Milan 1990, pp. 187, 189, 191.

26.

MICHELANGELO

Study for the Doorway from the Vestibule to the Reading Room of the Laurentian Library, circa 1526
Pen and brown watercolor washes on paper, 13½ x 9⅜ inches
inv. 98A

These two drawings in the artist's hand (cats. 26 and 27) represent preliminary designs for the two doorways in the Laurentian Library leading from the stairs to the Reading Room and vice versa. The careful execution of the drawings suggests that these are "models," made to be shown to Pope Clement VII for his approval. The doorways are outlined very clearly—so much so that Michael Hirst described these drawings as a fine graphic parallel to the work in *pietra serena* that would be derived from them. Set in place in 1533, the room's inner doorway was carried out with a more complex solution than the initial design, while the outer doorway was somewhat simplified. Thus the sometimes-contested attribution of the two drawings to Michelangelo also seems credible in the light of formal evidence.

Michelangelo, Doorway from the Vestibule
to the Reading Room of the Medici
Laurentian Library, Florence

BIBLIOGRAPHY

Michael Hirst, *Michel-Ange dessinateur,* exhibition cat., Paris and Milan 1989, p. 78, no. 32.

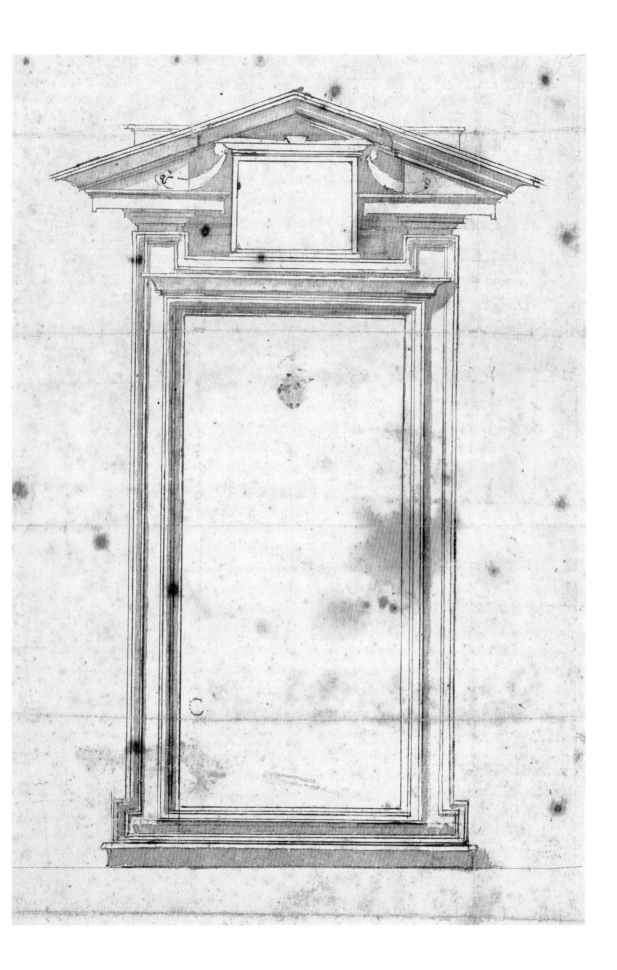

27.

MICHELANGELO

Study for the Doorway from the Reading Room to the Vestibule
of the Laurentian Library, circa 1526
Black pencil, pen, and brown watercolor washes on paper,
16 x 10 inches
inv. IIIA

Michelangelo, Doorway from the Reading Room to the
Vestibule of the Medici Laurentian Library, Florence

28.

MICHELANGELO

Study for the Ceiling of the Laurentian Library Reading Room, 1526
Black pencil and red pencil on paper, 14¾ x 8⅜ inches
inv. 126A

This study of ornamental designs for the ceiling of the Laurentian Library Reading Room shows a project that has arrived at an advanced state of elaboration. This can be seen in comparison to the earlier, more hesitant and summary sketch on the verso of Michelangelo's drawing in the Ashmolean Museum in Oxford, and especially in its affinity with the finished work.

The making of the wooden ceiling, decided upon between April and June 1526,

Ceiling of the Reading Room of the
Medici Laurentian Library, Florence

was carried out by Giovanni Battista del Tasso (1500–1555) and by Antonio di Marco di Giano, called il Carota (1485–1568). As witnessed by the inclusion of the coat of arms of Cosimo I—proclaimed Duke of Florence in 1537, when he had just turned eighteen—the ceiling was not made before this date but probably much later, between 1549 and 1550. In any case, in spite of the time lapse, the translation into wood does not diverge significantly from the master's indications. It does reduce the number of rectangular panels in the side compartments from three to two. The imaginative and unusually minute character of the ornamentation is in some ways stiffer than in Michelangelo's drawing, which seems to recall the stuccoed and painted grotesque elements that Giovanni da Udine had created in 1517 for the Palazzo Medici, erected just a short distance from the Laurentian complex.

BIBLIOGRAPHY

Charles de Tolnay, "Un 'pensiero' nuovo di Michelangelo per il soffitto della Libreria Laurenziana," in *Critica d'arte*, 1955, II, 9, pp. 237–240.

Paola Barocchi, *Michelangelo e la sua scuola. I disegni di Casa Buonarroti e degli Uffizi*, Florence 1962, pp. 115–116, no. 91.

Maria Ida Catalano, *Il pavimento della Biblioteca Medicea Laurenziana*, Florence 1992, pp. 12–14.

29.

MICHELANGELO

Study for a Reading Bench, with Seated Figure,
for the Laurentian Library, 1524–1525
Pen and red pencil on paper, 6¼ x 7¼ inches
inv. 94A

The Laurentian Library had been commissioned in 1519; however, at that time, Michelangelo was busy working on the New Sacristy, and so the Library construction wasn't begun until 1524, after the election of Pope Clement VII. Once the solution had been found as to where to locate the new building within the Laurentian complex, the foundations, external buttresses, and the installation of the Reading Room were carried out between 1524 and 1525. Although it was still premature to think about the interior decoration, we know that, already in those years, Clement VII had it on his mind to the point that, in 1524, he asked news, through one of Michelangelo's correspondents, of how the artist was thinking of making the benches for the Reading Room. This drawing is one of the artist's first ideas on this subject.

Conceived between 1524 and 1533, the benches were only officially commissioned in August of 1533 and their realization begun the following year, after Michelangelo had already left for Rome, never to return. Their making was entrusted to mediocre hands, and so they were covered with insignificant decorations. This drawing shows, however, that the builders respected the structure that the master had indicated—probably many years earlier—since the bench form was precisely connected with the articulation of the room's walls. The outline of a reader, seen on the right, is certainly by Michelangelo's hand, while there are still many doubts about the red pencil sketches that can be seen on the left side of the paper.

BIBLIOGRAPHY

Paola Barocchi, *Michelangelo e la sua scuola. I disegni di Casa Buonarroti e degli Uffizi*, Florence 1962, I, pp. 114–115, no. 90.

30

MICHELANGELO

Design for a Fortification at the Gate of Prato d'Ognissanti, circa 1529–1530
Pen, red pencil, and watercolor on paper, 16⅛ x 22⅜ inches
inv. 13A

In the first months of 1529, alarming news spread through Florence: it was reported that Pope Clement VII was preparing, with the aid of imperial troops, to bring his family back to power after they had been driven from the city on May 17 two years earlier. The Popular Government decided to complete the works for the city's defense, which had been begun under the Medici in 1526 but had been left incomplete. A committee, the "Militia Nine," was formed, and Michelangelo was called to take part; soon thereafter he would be nominated "governor and general executor of the fortifications." Invested with such an important responsibility and encouraged by his fellow citizens' esteem, Michelangelo elaborated a series of proposals for the defense of the city gates. However, on account of their complexity and novelty, his ideas went unrealized. Although a small portion of his plans may have been carried out, no evidence of construction exists today. For this reason, it is only possible to reconstruct his projects for the fortifications through the study of the twenty-odd extraordinary drawings belonging to the Casa Buonarroti. These designs for fortifications were well known at Louis XIV's court, because they were studied by the Marquis of Vauban; they were then documented in various hands at the beginning of the twentieth century. Still, it wasn't until much more recent times that these drawings were fully appreciated.

We can see today a great originality in the drawings, a dynamic expression that is in full accord with Michelangelo's architecture of the same period, as well as with his tactical and strategic innovations. It is certain that the artist's contemporaries remained unaware of the operational validity of these projects. To emphasize their efficacy today does not detract in any way from the aesthetic quality of these drawings. A particularly felicitous example is drawing 13A, which is famed among scholars for its communicative beauty. It was described by Paola Barocchi as an "invention . . . that opens and breaks, with an expanding energy that leaves the imprint of its own spatial axes on the surrounding environment."

The City Gate at Prato d'Ognissanti in Florence toward the end
of the fifteenth century (from the "Chain Map," circa 1472)

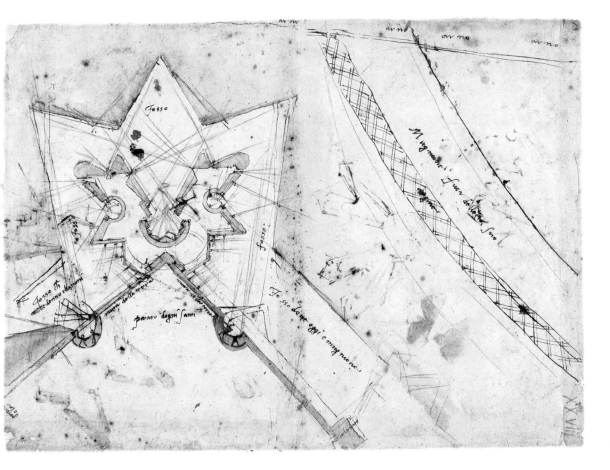

BIBLIOGRAPHY

Paola Barocchi, *Michelangelo e la sua scuola. I disegni di Casa Buonarroti e degli Uffizi,* Florence 1962, I, pp. 141–143, no. 114.

Pietro C. Marani, *Disegni di fortificazioni da Leonardo a Michelangelo,* exhibition cat., Casa Buonarroti, Florence 1984, pp. 69–70, 79, nos. 36, 51.

Giulio Carlo Argan and Bruno Contardi, *Michelangelo architetto,* Milan 1990, pp. 145–153, 202–209.

The Sistine Chapel (exterior), Vatican City

MICHELANGELO AND
THE SISTINE CHAPEL IN ROME

Speaking on the controversial topic of the primacy of the arts, Benedetto Varchi concluded his famous *lezzione* (lesson), held at the Accademia Fiorentina in 1547, by conferring equal merit to painting and sculpture. He based his judgment on the observation that the two arts share the same objectives and are differentiated only by incidental elements.

The author sent his text to Michelangelo, who confirmed its receipt in an ironic letter; here we can quote several passages that convey the artist's attitude with regard to the two arts. In his letter Michelangelo says that, for him, sculpture seems better "the more it tends towards relief" and that "relief seems poor the more it moves towards painting." Moreover he declares, "I take sculpture to be that which is taken away by force; that which is made through addition is similar to painting." This axiom, borrowed from Neoplatonic tradition, clearly explains the obstinate preference of an artist who would always declare himself and sign his work "Michelangelo sculptor." Vasari tells of Michelangelo as a thirteen-year-old apprentice in the workshop of painters Domenico and Davide Ghirlandaio, an apprenticeship that was supposed to last three years but ended after a few months (a document published in 1993 moves this presence up by one year); and the biographer describes at length Domenico's astonishment at the proof of his young pupil's extraordinary graphic abilities. But Ascanio Condivi, to please his master, skims over all this, to evoke instead the image of an artist who, ever since the beginning, followed a powerful, irrepressible, independent vocation; an artist who let himself, however, be taken in hand by a slightly older friend, Francesco Granacci, in order to become a member of the circle of the Garden of San Marco. Here artists studied the lessons of antiquity through the collections of classical statues, and became sculptors under the tutelage of the elderly sculptor Bertoldo di Giovanni. For his own part, Michelangelo felt that his brief experience in the Ghirlandaio workshop was of little importance; by contrast the image of the artist forever devoted to sculpture corresponds to the historical truth of the extraordinary cultural and artistic experience that Michelangelo lived in the Medici Garden.

So he began as a sculptor, and always continued to define himself as such, even during the most exalted and dramatic moments of his great painting project in the Sistine Chapel. Yet, as has often and rightly been pointed out, among Michelangelo's most complex and grandiose projects, he succeeded in carrying out the paintings whereas his work as a sculptor either became the torment of a lifetime (i.e., the tomb of Julius II) or concealed, behind the sublime character of a masterpiece, his bitterness at having to renounce more elaborate ideas (the greatest example of this is the New Sacristy for San Lorenzo).

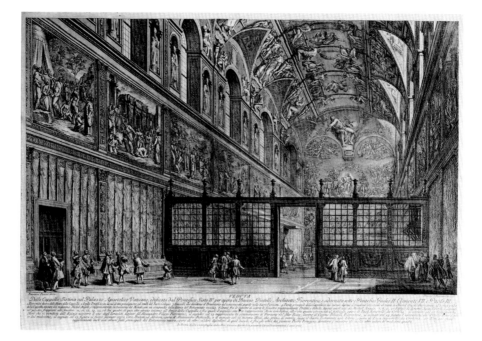

Francesco Barbazza (from a drawing by Francesco Panini), *View of the Sistine Chapel,*
Florence, Casa Buonarroti, inv. 543

We can trace the first episodes of that long and bitter struggle, which, right
from the beginning, Michelangelo referred to as "the tragedy of the tomb": in 1505
the approval of his project for the tomb of Julius II (Pope from 1503 to 1513); the
artist's initial enthusiasm and the eight months spent quarrying marble in Carrara; the
repeal of his commission by the Pope and the artist's subsequent indignant flight
from Rome in 1506; these events were to overshadow the beginnings of the decoration project for the Sistine Chapel ceiling. The Pope's change of mind can be explained by the fact that he was engaged in financing military actions against Perugia
and Bologna and that he was also anxious to build, with Bramante (circa 1444–1514),
the new basilica of Saint Peter. It should not be imagined that Julius wanted to do
justice to a wronged artist by entrusting him with another important project: in fact,
the papal decision to commission the ceiling decoration from Michelangelo preceded,
albeit by only a few days, his dramatic flight. In the context of these complicated
events, the only aspect that clearly stands out is Michelangelo's disappointment and
his reluctance, as witnessed by his biographers and his papers, to accept a job that over
the years he would continue to declare "not to be [his] profession." At first the artist
flatly refused to do the project, moved by disdain as well as by the idea of having to
abandon his congenial work with marble for a painting project of such great dimensions, something he had never attempted before. His design for the *Battle of Cascina*—
the fresco that had been meant to decorate one of the walls of the Sala del Maggior
Consiglio in the Palazzo Vecchio in Florence—had never gone beyond the phase of
the preparatory cartoon; the other paintings of his youth—among them, the
Uffizi's *Doni Tondo,* unanimously attributed to his hand, and the London National
Gallery's *Manchester Madonna,* a recent and authoritative attribution—were carried out
on medium-sized panels.

There followed, but not until two years later, a forced reconciliation in Bologna
with the Pope, whose insistence, with time, took the form of an order. On May 10,
1508, Michelangelo received a first payment and began to work; he was thirty-three
years old. He must have begun with drawings and cartoons since it is documented
that the scaffolding was built and the plaster applied between May 11 and July 27

Michelangelo, *Initial Study for the Vault of the Sistine Chapel*, London, British Museum,
Department of Prints and Drawings, inv. 1859-6-25-567

(the date on which these preliminary operations were paid). The fresco work was then
carried forward without interruptions until half the ceiling was complete (1510), only
to be picked up again and, as we shall see, completed two years later.

It is worthwhile to pause and consider what the Sistine Chapel looked like
when Michelangelo saw it for the first time. (This was probably not during his first
stay in Rome between 1495 and 1501 but only sometime between 1505 and 1506.)
Built—or more precisely, renovated from a preexisting "Cappella Magna" or Great
Chapel—by Sixtus IV (Pope from 1471 to 1484), the chapel at the turn of the new
century must have appeared much as it has been described by Ernst Steinmann in his
well-known reconstruction. It should be remembered that the Chapel was one of the
most important places in the Vatican buildings: for instance, it was here that conclaves
met to elect the new Pope. Even today the Chapel's exterior appearance is massive,
like a fortress.

The fresco decoration commissioned by Sixtus IV, with scenes of Christ and
Moses and portraits of twenty-four pontiffs, had been carried out between 1481 and
1483 by painters such as Perugino, Sandro Botticelli, Domenico Ghirlandaio, Cosimo
Rosselli and their assistants, among them Pinturicchio, Luca Signorelli and Bartolo-
meo della Gatta. These paintings originally ran around the four sides, with Perugino's
Assumption of the Virgin on the end wall, above the altar. (In fact, the Chapel itself was
consecrated to the mystery of the Assumption.) It was on this wall that years later
Michelangelo would paint his *Last Judgment.* Following an old iconographic tradition,
Pier Matteo d'Amelia had painted the ceiling as a large starry sky.

Initially Michelangelo's idea was to do away with the starry sky and to arrange,
in the vault's corbels, the figures of the twelve apostles; the rest would be decorated
with geometrical partitions and elaborate frames, following a model derived from
ancient ceilings and made popular at the time by Pinturicchio's workshop. But this
solution—of which there is still evidence in a drawing belonging to the British
Museum—soon proved inadequate to him. This fact is recalled in a letter that
Michelangelo wrote many years later, in December 1523, to Giovanfrancesco Fattucci.
In it he tells of his dissatisfaction with that early project of making "only the

Raphael Sanzio, *School of Athens*, Vatican City, Stanza della Segnatura

apostles," which seemed to him destined to result in "a poor thing." The same letter also documents a succinct dialogue: when the Pope asked him why he felt this way about the idea for the apostles, the artist replied, "because they, too, were poor." This sentence, Michelangelo continues, convinced Julius II, who then gave the artist free rein on the project.

It is truly striking to consider the contrast between the anecdote's humility and what happened afterwards: that is, the realization of a spatial and aesthetic concept that would leave an indelible mark on the history of art, sweeping aside so much of what had gone before. There is still much discussion on how much freedom Michelangelo was allowed in terms of the complicated iconographic program that he adopted for the ceiling; however, it seems highly probable that he asked for help and advice from theologians at the papal court. This cyclopean representation certainly didn't excite the violent reactions which, in the climate of the Counter-Reformation, accompanied the origins and inauguration of the *Last Judgment*. The freedom allowed the artist was expressed not so much in the choice of subject matter, which in any case had to conform to certain parameters since this was a place where the most solemn liturgies were celebrated, but rather in the famous and revolutionary arrangement that places the ceiling figures above the grandiose scheme of painted architecture.

While Michelangelo was busy on the Sistine Chapel scaffolding, just a short distance away Raphael was beginning to decorate the room known as the Stanza della Segnatura. The foundations of Italian art were being overturned, once and for all, even though the artists' contemporaries were perhaps not fully aware of the extraordinary significance of these events.

The break with fifteenth-century tradition was exceptional not only on a formal level; it also required the work to be organized in completely different ways from the workshop practices that had been in use. Almost immediately, Michelangelo saw that the assistants his friend Granacci had procured would not be suitable, even though

Michelangelo, Sistine Chapel Ceiling, Vatican City

some of the artists called from Florence were well known, like Giuliano Bugiardini or Aristotele da Sangallo. The artist faced the gigantic project alone, keeping by his side only a few assistants who were given menial tasks. For more than four years, with the exception of a few very brief intervals, Michelangelo painted standing up or lying down, but always with his head looking upward, a position that is so tiring and un- natural that, for several months after the work had been completed, he had to place everything that he needed to read or look at carefully over his head. The artist portrayed himself, intent on his arduous task, in an ironic sketch found in the mar- gins of a sonnet, preserved in the Buonarroti Archive and displayed in this exhibition (see cat. 31).

The ceiling decoration took place, as we have seen, in two phases: from the summer of 1508 to 1510, the first half was carried out, up to and including the *Creation of Eve*. Michelangelo began painting above the Chapel door, moving in the direction of the altar in order to allow liturgical activity to continue during the early phase of work. This is why the scenes that were painted first correspond to the end of the icono- graphic series: that is to say, in his realization of the project, the artist worked from the scenes of Noah back to those of the Creation. The scaffolding for the second half of the ceiling was built in the spring of 1511, and the work continued quickly until its conclusion in late October 1512. In the continuity of painted architecture that supports the entire composition, we see, in the second phase, a progressive increase of drama while the figures are larger and the compositions seem to be more freely arranged. At the same time, the use of gold, one of the last reminders of Quattro- cento workshops, was reduced almost to nonexistence.

The history of the sixteenth-century decoration of the Sistine Chapel includes various other episodes apart from the painting of the ceiling and the abrupt jump that takes us to the period of the *Last Judgment.* Among these we should keep in mind Raphael's cartoons of *Scenes of Saint Peter and Saint Paul* for the tapestries used on solemn occasions to cover the lower part of the walls, overlaying the trompe l'oeil curtains that had been painted there during the time of Sixtus IV. These tapestries, woven in Brussels, were presented for the first time on December 26, 1519.

Michelangelo, *Study for the Last Judgment*, Florence, Casa Buonarroti, inv. 65F

Michelangelo, *Last Judgment*, Vatican City, Sistine Chapel

View of the Sistine Chapel, Vatican City

Michelangelo's next project for the Sistine Chapel began in 1536 when, twenty-four years after his completion of the ceiling decoration, the artist—then in his sixties—undertook the painting of the wall behind the altar. The work had been commissioned to the artist by Clement VII in 1533, and after the Pope's death it was confirmed by his successor Paul III. As has been mentioned other times in these pages, Michelangelo, in order to carry out this commission (and also attracted to Rome by his affection for Tommaso dei Cavalieri), left Florence, never to return.

The great wall above the altar was not, however, completely bare: on it, as we have seen, Perugino had painted his *Assumption.* Moreover, there were two other episodes of the fifteenth-century cycle (depicting the parallel stories of the finding of Moses and the birth of Christ) as well as several effigies of pontiffs and, in the two lunettes above, several of Christ's ancestors, which Michelangelo himself had painted while working on the ceiling. At first the artist tried not to destroy the preexisting decoration completely, taking special care to preserve Perugino's work, to whose subject the Chapel was dedicated. There is eloquent proof of this found in a famous drawing in the Casa Buonarroti Collection: in the lower center, one can clearly see that the fifteenth-century altarpiece has been set apart by a frame while, by contrast, the souls of the damned are seen writhing around it. From the same drawing we can gather that, already at this early stage, the artist had clearly in his mind the

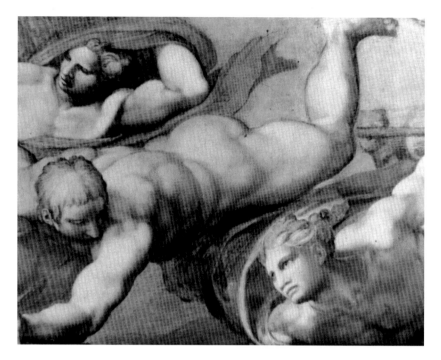

Michelangelo, *Last Judgment* (detail), Vatican City, Sistine Chapel

Michelangelo, *Last Judgment* (detail with
self-portrait), Vatican City, Sistine Chapel

Michelangelo, *Last Judgment* (detail with Judging Christ), Vatican City, Sistine Chapel

Michelangelo, *Battle of the Centaurs* (detail), Florence, Casa Buonarroti, inv. 194

composition's complex dynamic, with Christ the Judge serving as the powerful impetus for almost the entire action. We can see Michelangelo's still-vivid memory of his youthful work, the *Battle of the Centaurs,* whose central figure is mirrored in the pose of Christ the Judge.

Inevitably, Michelangelo soon gave up trying to save Perugino's altarpiece and began a decoration starting from a fresh layer of plaster. It is clear that all forms of illusionism have been abandoned in the *Judgment;* the powerful scansions present in the ceiling work are absent here, while the strong blue of the lapis lazuli background denies and does away with the serene perspectival conquests of the Quattrocento. In the immense scene, the bodies stay heavily afloat in the air, through the strength of their muscles, in an uninterrupted and slow circular movement; they are denied the aid of wings, which were eliminated even in the angel figures, a fact that caused much scandal among contemporaries, by then steeped in the Counter-Reformation ethic. During this project, the artist, no longer young, went through frequent bouts of black moods, as can be seen in his famous self-portrait on the flayed skin which Saint Bartholomew holds in his hand; moreover the saint's features identify him as Pietro Aretino, a man of letters who in those years had become Michelangelo's bitter adversary. There is no end to the violations of the traditional iconography used for the *Last Judgment:* one of the most obvious is the boat oared by Charon, the mythological ferryman of souls, which the artist picked up from the *Divine Comedy,* Dante Alighieri's poem that Michelangelo loved deeply.

When the *Last Judgment* was inaugurated on November 1, 1541, there was great disconcertment and immeasurable criticism addressed especially to the iconographic anomalies we have already mentioned as well as to the great number of nude figures. The work risked being completely destroyed, but by that time Michelangelo's great fame was such that the damage was limited to covering the nudity and to the destruction and repainting of a few figures. This intervention was carried out by Daniele da Volterra, Michelangelo's pupil and friend, who in this way contributed, perhaps knowingly, to preserving the masterpiece.

The time was 1565, just one year after Michelangelo's death.

31.

MICHELANGELO

Self-Portrait in the Act of Painting the Sistine Chapel Ceiling
(with a Sonnet in the Artist's Handwriting), 1508–1512
Pen, 11½ x 7⅞ inches
Buonarroti Archive, XIII, folio 111

This playful self-portrait was already admired and studied during Michelangelo the Younger's times. In spite of its popularity, we can say that until a few years ago the fate of Michelangelo's drawings preserved in the precious volumes of the Buonarroti Archive were indeed modest when compared to their great aesthetic value. For a long time the artistic worth of the papers was considered secondary to their documentary value, since they provided biographers and scholars with indispensable testimony that helped clear up the artist's often tangled biography.

The attention devoted to these drawings remained occasional—with the exceptions of Frey, Thode, and Berenson—until Charles de Tolnay wrote his essay published in the "Münchner Jahrbuch der Bildenden Kunst" in 1928. In this text, de Tolnay was the first to perform a systematic investigation of the graphic material contained in the Buonarroti Archive and to discuss it in the general light of Michelangelo's artistic output. De Tolnay made some acute observations about this drawing: "The sketch is not a realistic self-portrait or a descriptive caricature, but only an abbreviated indication of the content of the verses in a concise diagram. Without the verses the sketch would not have its full artistic effect, but when the sonnet has been read, it synthesizes the meaning."

And truly the sonnet and the drawn image complete each other as Michelangelo traces here his own double portrait, describing his precarious physical condition resulting from the unnatural position he had been forced to hold for painting the Sistine Chapel ceiling. In this message to his friend Giovanni da Pistoia, Michelangelo uses the power of words and images to describe the difficult working conditions: he is seen here standing up on the scaffolding with his head back and his right arm extended upward.

However, it is with light-hearted irony that Michelangelo describes a reality that, as his biographers tell, caused him trouble for a long time afterward. Indeed, this is confirmed by Ascanio Condivi, the artist's pupil as well as author of the *Life of Michelangelo Buonarroti* (1553), which was inspired and—contrary to Vasari's biography—approved by the master himself. Condivi wrote that Michelangelo, after having concluded his great and solitary undertaking of the Sistine Chapel ceiling, "on account of having painted such a long time keeping his eyes raised towards the ceiling, couldn't see very well when he looked down so that if he had to read a letter or study some tiny thing, he had to hold it up with his arms over his head."

BIBLIOGRAPHY

Paola Barocchi, *Michelangelo e la sua scuola. I disegni dell'Archivio Buonarroti*, Florence 1964, pp. V–VIII, 6–8, n. 288.

I o gia facto ūgozo ī questo stēto
Chome fa lacqua agacti ī lonbardia
ouer daltro paese chessi chesisia
cha forza luētre apicha soctolmēto

L a barba alcielo ellamemoria sento
ī sullo scrignio e lpecto fo darpia
e lpennel sopraluiso tuctauia
melfa gocciando ū richo pauimēto

E lōbi entrati miso nella peccia
e fo delcul p chotrapeso groppa
e passi seza ghochi muouo īuano

D i māzi misalluga lachorteccia
e p piegarsi adietro sira groppa
e tēdomi comarcho soriano

Po fallaci e strano
surgie iliuditio ēs lamēte porta
ch mal sipra p cerboctana torta
lamia pictura morta

di fedi orma giouanni elmio onore
nō sedo ī lo g bō ne io pictore

32.

MICHELANGELO

Studies of Nudes and the Cornice, for the Sistine Chapel Ceiling, 1508–1509
Black pencil and pen, 16⅜ x 10¾ inches
inv. 75F

Michelangelo probably undertook the immense task of decorating the Sistine Chapel ceiling in the early autumn of 1508. Indeed the images drawn on this interesting and busy sheet can be dated more or less to this period. Probably the first drawing made here was the study for a cornice decorated with acorn and shell motifs taken from the coat of arms of the Della Rovere family from Savona, of which the commissioning Pope Julius II was a member. This motif was not used for the ceiling's great cornice, which remained free of decorative elements and inspired by classical models, giving a more monumental effect. This motif can be found, using a simpler modelling, in the frames that surround the crests and lunettes.

Right from the beginning Michelangelo planned to insert figures, the so-called Nudes, in the ceiling decoration. On this page we can recognize the study for the Nude located to the left of the Cumaean Sibyl as well as for the one to the right of the Prophet Jeremiah. The smaller sketches are found to contain the first inspirations for the Nude to the right of the Prophet Isaiah.

Vitality, dynamic research, originality in the sign are the undoubted qualities of this drawing, so that they lead most critics to suspect that it is completely by the master's hand. Frey and Barocchi, however, have expressed strong doubts about the parts of the page where the pencil has been gone over in ink.

Michelangelo, Sistine Chapel Ceiling
(detail with *Nude to the right of the
Prophet Jeremiah*), Vatican City

Michelangelo, Sistine Chapel Ceiling
(detail with *Nude to the left of the
Cumaean Sibyl*), Vatican City

BIBLIOGRAPHY

Paola Barocchi, *Michelangelo e la sua scuola. I disegni di Casa Buonarroti e degli Uffizi*, Florence 1962, pp. 24–26.
Michael Hirst, *Michelangelo and his Drawings*, New Haven and London 1988, pp. 35, 91.

33.

MICHELANGELO

Study of a Man's Face, for the Sistine Chapel Ceiling, 1509–1510
Red pencil, 5 x 5⅝ inches
inv. 47F

This study of a man's head, with his intense expression of concentration, can be dated—on the basis of stylistic evidence—to the years of Michelangelo's work on the Sistine Chapel. It has been ascribed to two figures in the scene of the Flood: one holding a baby, on the right, and the other, on the left, portrayed in the act of climbing up a tree.

The half profile is slightly bent forward and the eyelids are lowered in a manner that suggests this drawing may have been inspired by a death mask.

Michelangelo, Sistine Chapel Ceiling
(detail of *The Flood*), Vatican City

34.

MICHELANGELO

Study of Adam Driven from Paradise, for the Sistine Chapel Ceiling, circa 1510
Black pencil, 10⅜ x 7⅝ inches
inv. 45F

Aurelio Gotti, Director of the Florentine Royal Galleries and biographer of Michelangelo, described this drawing in 1875: "Sketch, in black pencil, of a male nude, turned slightly to the right in a pose of fear; the head and part of the legs have not been done. An idea for the fresco of Adam Driven from Earthly Paradise painted on the Sistine Chapel Ceiling in Rome."

The drawing, of excellent quality, appeared to Paola Barocchi the expression of a rather mature idea, carried out with an "almost greater" fullness than the corresponding figure painted on the Chapel ceiling. Michael Hirst efficaciously emphasizes, in this drawing, the rapidity of the sign that reveals the approach to the problem of capturing the human body's plasticity once the fundamental idea of the figure has been established and the artist is conditioned by the movement that he himself has chosen.

Michelangelo, Sistine Chapel Ceiling (detail of
Expulsion from Paradise), Vatican City

BIBLIOGRAPHY

Aurelio Gotti, *Vita di Michelangelo Buonarroti narrata con l'aiuto di nuovi documenti*, II, Florence 1875, p. 191.

Paola Barocchi, *Michelangelo e la sua scuola. I disegni di Casa Buonarroti e degli Uffizi*, Florence 1962, p. 28, n. 18.

Michael Hirst, *Michelangelo and His Drawings*, New Haven and London 1988, pp. 27, 61.

35.

MICHELANGELO

Study of an Arm for the Sistine Chapel Ceiling, 1509–1510
Black pencil, ⅜ x 5⅛ inches
inv. 8F

The rather energetic marking, exalted by the plastic use of chiaroscuro, has prompted Luciano Berti to define (in this as in other similar youthful works) the technique that Michelangelo uses here as "drawing by sculpting." He sees in this drawing a probable memory of the ancient *Discus Thrower* but above all a powerful hand related to a motif explored in the *David* and repeatedly present in the figures of the Sistine Chapel ceiling. It is not by chance that critics have ascribed this right forearm—extended horizontally and charged with vitality, in spite of its static position—to different figures: Frey, for instance, sees it as the arm of God the Father in the *Creation of Adam,* while Wilde and de Tolnay refer to it as the mirror opposite of drunken Noah's left arm. Thode believed the drawing belonged to the much later period of the *Last Judgment,* but most scholars agree that it exhibits the salient characteristics of the young artist's style and spirituality when he was still sculpting the *David* and beginning the Sistine Chapel project.

Michelangelo, Sistine Chapel Ceiling (detail of *The Creation of Adam*), Vatican City

Michelangelo, Sistine Chapel Ceiling (detail of *The Drunkenness of Noah*), Vatican City

BIBLIOGRAPHY

Paola Barocchi, *Michelangelo e la sua scuola. I disegni di Casa Buonarroti e degli Uffizi,* Florence 1962, p. 31, n. 20.

Luciano Berti, *Michelangelo. I disegni di Casa Buonarroti,* Florence 1985, p. 14.

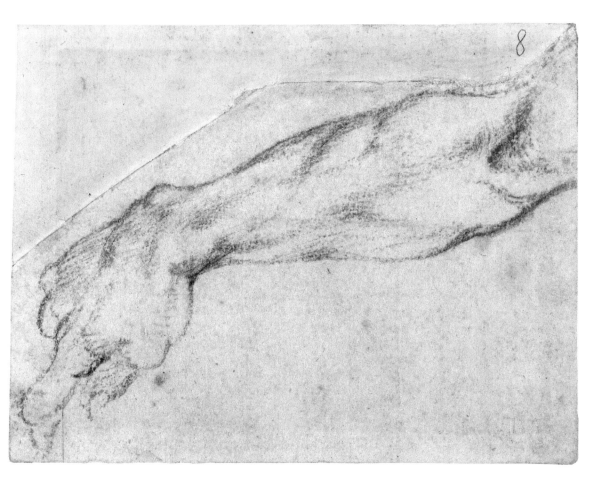

8

36.

MICHELANGELO

Study of a Resurrected Christ, circa 1532
Black pencil, 13 x 7¾ inches
inv. 66F

This drawing has a particular and highly communicative immediate quality: its light, barely visible chiaroscuro, and the overlapping of the *pentimenti* in fact contribute to exalting the dynamic force of a body captured in the moment when it is about to twist around on itself. The ingenious invention—the artist's hand has been recognized almost unanimously by critics—has been attributed to the Christ figure in the *Last Judgment,* but also, and perhaps this is a more believable hypothesis, to studies of Resurrection figures predating the Sistine Chapel walls. Here Michelangelo seems to be still engaged in investigating complex compositional modules, which only later would reach the plastic and daring power of the *Judgment.* The theme of the Resurrection of Christ held Michelangelo's interest for a rather long period which Wilde has dated between 1532 and 1533. There are remarkable stylistic similarities between this drawing and the ones like the 61F in the Casa Buonarotti Collection or the 691 bis belonging to the Louvre.

Michelangelo, *Study for a Resurrected Christ,*
Florence, Casa Buonarroti, inv. 61F

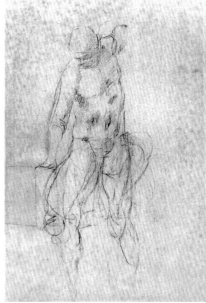

Michelangelo, *Resurrection of Christ,*
Paris, Louvre, Département des Arts
Graphiques, inv. 691 bis

BIBLIOGRAPHY

Paola Barocchi, *Michelangelo e la sua scuola. I disegni di Casa Buonarroti e degli Uffizi,* Florence 1962, pp. 169–170, n. 136.

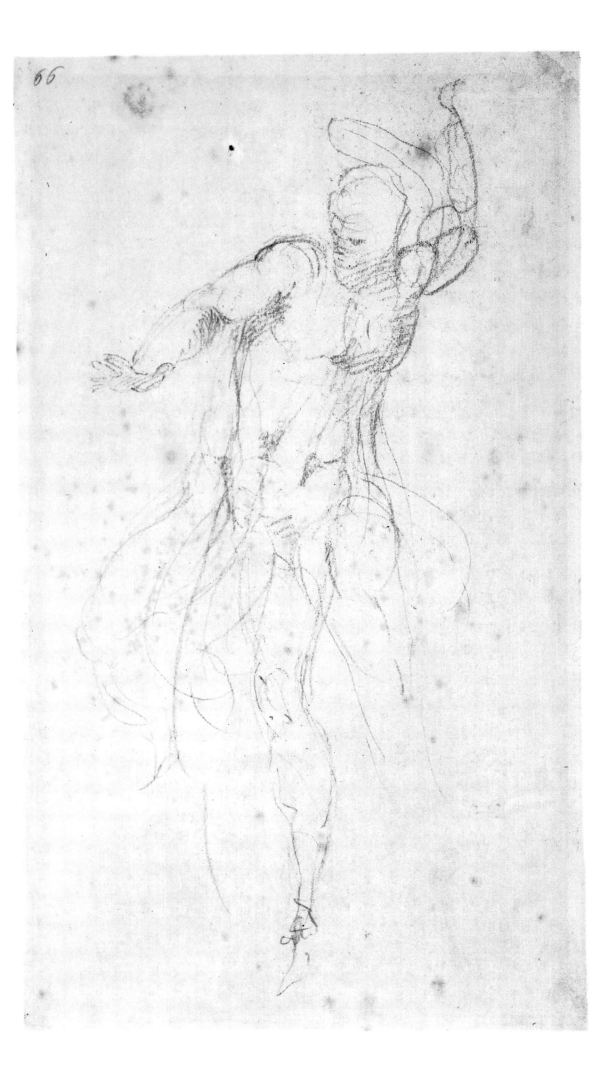

37.

CIRCLE OF GIULIO CLOVIO (1498–1578)
Last Judgment (after Michelangelo), circa 1570
Parchment, 12⅝ x 9 inches
inv. Gallerie 1890, n. 810

This miniature came from the Medici collections at the Uffizi to the Casa Buonarroti in the 1930s. The parchment depicts the Sistine Chapel's *Last Judgment*, with all its three hundred and ninety-one figures and without any of the famous additions of censorship to which the original had been subjected. Here all the original nudes can be seen, including the group that created the greatest scandal: Saint Biagio, with brushes in hand, who observes Saint Catherine on her wheel of martyrdom (on the far right, halfway up the composition). This group was not only "trousered" but was even completely repainted by Daniele da Volterra in 1565.

According to Giovanni Agosti, this miniature recalls the engraving executed from the *Judgment* in 1569 by Dalmatian artist Martino Rota, however indirectly and referring to evidence that clearly predated 1565. The small variations are, however, significant: for instance, Christ is given back his beard, the absence of which in the fresco had been strongly criticized. At the top of the composition, where Rota in his engraving had set a portrait of Michelangelo, in the miniature version we see depicted, in obedience to Counter-Reformation prescriptions, representations of God and the Holy Spirit. The work's stylistic characteristics ascribe it to Giulio Clovio, the most important miniaturist of the sixteenth century.

BIBLIOGRAPHY

Giovanni Agosti, "Un Giudizio Universale in miniatura," in *Annali della Scuola Normale Superiore di Pisa*, s. III, XIX, 4, 1989, pp. 1291–1297.

38–47.

GIORGIO GHISI (1520–1582)
Last Judgment (after Michelangelo), 1545–1550
Engraving (ten sheets)
inv. 563

A great number of engravings were made after Michelangelo's works and published in the second half of the sixteenth century. These prints were often
mediocre in quality and were multiplied through the avidity of engravers
deemed by Giorgio Vasari to be "attracted more by profit than by honor." In 1568 Vasari,
in his biography of Marcantonio Raimondi, placed this *Judgment* by Ghisi among the
few engravings worthy of being saved. Indeed the work has enjoyed great notoriety
over the centuries, due in part to the most salient characteristic: it is composed of
ten sheets, marked by the letters of the alphabet from A to L, which, when mounted
together, constitute a complete reproduction of the Sistine Chapel fresco. Further
proof of the popularity of this version of the *Judgment* is seen in its nine editions, as
well as in the fact that its plates still exist today, preserved in the Istituto Nazionale

Giorgio Ghisi, *Last Judgment* (after Michelangelo),
detail of *Charon's Boat*, with dedication to Mathys
van de Merwede, Florence, Casa Buonarroti, inv. 563

per la Grafica (National Institute for Graphic Arts) in
Rome. They arrived there
from the Calcografia Cam-
erale (Parliamentary Institute
of Engraving), whose stamp
marks the Casa Buonarroti
engravings, taken from the
reprint made by engraver
Giovanni Giacomo de' Rossi
(1627–1691). Here the folio I
shows, under Charon's boat,
a dedication to Mathys van
de Merwede, Lord of Cloot-
wyck, a patron of artists who
was in Italy between 1647 and 1650. This dedication substitutes the written text exalting Michelangelo that had been included in all the previous editions. The series of
engravings currently on display was printed on plates that had undergone heavy ma-
nipulation in 1823 when the nude figures were covered by more drapery and shading.

Here, as in other famous prints by his hand, Ghisi reveals his refined engraving
technique, which he had learned first through studying drawing in Mantova with
Giulio Romano; then in Rome, fully embracing Marcantonio Raimondi's lessons; yet
not disdaining, during his stay in Antwerp, the dictates of the Flemish engraving
school, which devoted such close attention to Michelangelo's models.

Alida Molteda gave a fine definition of his mastery when she affirmed that here
"the engraver tries to go beyond a mere iconographic report of the image in order to
try to pin-point the overall sense of the same, divided into groups, but at the same
time sustained by a unique dynamic force."

Abundantly copied right from the beginning, even in single sheets, Ghisi's
Judgment found its most famous copier in the sixteenth-century French engraver
Nicolaus Beatrizet, who faithfully reproduced the single lines while giving his own
work a personal touch, particularly with regard to the figures' physiognomic features.

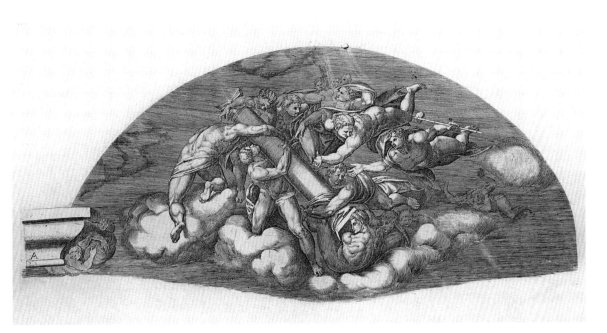

Lunette with Symbols of the Passion, 9½ x 20½ inches

Lunette with Symbols of the Passion, 8¼ x 21 inches

BIBLIOGRAPHY

Alida Moltedo, *La Sistina riprodotta,* exhibition cat., Rome 1991, pp. 68–72, n. 17.

Indice delle stampe De' Rossi. Contributo alla storia di una Stamperia romana, edited by Anna Grelle Iusco, Rome 1996, p. 449.

Group of Martyrs and Saints, 17¼ x 17⅛ inches

Christ the Judge with Virgin and Saints, 17⅜ x 19 inches

Group of Blessed Women, 15⅜ x 10⅞ inches

Struggle between Angels and the Damned, 12½ x 15¾ inches

Trumpet-Playing Angels, 13⅝ x 12¼ inches

Blessed Souls and Angels, 17⅛ x 16¾ inches

Charon's Boat, 14 x 21 inches

Group of Resurrected Souls, 12¼ x 22½ inches

BIBLIOGRAPHY OF REFERENCES

Giovanni Agosti, "Un Giudizio Universale in miniatura," in *Annali della Scuola Normale Superiore di Pisa*, s. III, XIX, 4, 1989.

Giovanni Agosti and Vincenzo Farinella, *Michelangelo e l'arte classica*, exhibition cat., Casa Buonarroti, Florence 1987.

Alessandro Alinari, in *Ceramica toscana dal Medioevo al XVII secolo*, edited by Gian Carlo Boiani, exhibition cat., Rome 1990.

Alessandro Angelini, in *Arte e Storia in Biblioteca*, edited by Stefano Corsi and Elena Lombardi, exhibition cat., Casa Buonarroti, Milan 1995.

Giulio Carlo Argan and Bruno Contardi, *Michelangelo architetto*, Milan 1990.

Ferdinando Arisi, *Gian Paolo Panini*, Milan 1961.

————, *Gian Paolo Panini e i fasti della Roma del 1700*, Rome 1986.

Philip Attwood, in *The Currency of Fame: Medals of the Renaissance*, edited by Stephen K. Scher, exhibition cat., New York 1994.

Benedetta Ballico, in *L'Accademia Etrusca*, exhibition cat., Milan 1985.

Paola Barocchi, *Michelangelo e la sua scuola. I disegni di Casa Buonarroti e degli Uffizi*, 2 vols., Florence 1962.

————, *Michelangelo e la sua scuola. I disegni dell'Archivio Buonarroti*, Florence 1964.

Luciano Berti, *Michelangelo. I disegni di Casa Buonarroti*, Alessandro Cecchi and Antonio Natali, Florence 1985.

Filippo Buonarroti, *Osservazioni istoriche sopra alcuni medaglioni antichi*, Rome 1698.

Michelangelo Buonarroti the Younger, *La Fiera e la Tancia*, edited by Anton Maria Salvini, Florence 1726.

————, *La Fiera. Redazione originaria (1619)*, edited by Umberto Limentani, Florence 1984.

Howard Burns, "San Lorenzo in Florence before the Building of the New Sacristy: an Early Plan," in *Mitteilungen des Kunsthistorischen Institutes in Florenz*, XXIII, 1979.

Il Carteggio di Michelangelo, edited by Paola Barocchi and Renzo Ristori, 5 vols., Florence 1965–1983.

Maria Ida Catalano, *Il pavimento della Biblioteca Medicea Laurenziana*, Florence 1992.

Antonio Cederna, *Mussolini urbanista. Lo sventramento di Roma negli anni del consenso*, Bari 1980.

Miles Chappell, *Cristofano Allori*, exhibition cat., Florence 1984.

Lucilla Bardeschi Ciulich, *Costanza ed evoluzione nella scrittura di Michelangelo*, exhibition cat., Casa Buonarroti, Florence 1989.

————, "I marmi di Michelangelo," in Marco Dezzi Bardeschi, *La difficile eredità. Architettura a Firenze dalla Repubblica all'assedio*, exhibition cat., Florence 1994.

————, *Michelangelo. Grafia e biografia di un genio*, exhibition cat., Milan 2000.

Ascanio Condivi, *Vita di Michelagnolo Buonarroti (1553)*, edited by Anton Francesco Gori, Florence 1746.

Stefano Corsi, *Casa Buonarroti. La collezione archeologica*, Milan 1997.

Carlo Del Bravo, "Su Cristofano Allori," in *Paragone* 205, 1967.

Charles de Tolnay, *Michelangelo*, 5 vols., Princeton 1947–1960.

————, "Un 'pensiero' nuovo di Michelangelo per il soffitto della Libreria Laurenziana," in *Critica d'arte*, 1955.

————, *L'omaggio a Michelangelo di Albrecht Dürer*, Rome 1972.

————, *Due lettere originali autografe di Michelangelo. Recenti acquisizioni delle collezioni della Casa Buonarroti*, in *Scritti in onore di Ugo Procacci*, II, Milan 1974.

————, *Corpus dei disegni di Michelangelo*, 4 vols., Novara 1975–1980.

Pier Luigi De Vecchi, *Michelangelo pittore*, Milan 1974.

Le due Cleopatre e le "teste divine" di Michelangelo, edited by Paola Barocchi, exhibition cat., Casa Buonarroti, Florence 1989.

Caroline Elam, "The Site and Early Building History of Michelangelo's New Sacristy," in *Mitteilungen des Kunsthistorischen Institutes in Florenz*, XXIII, 1979.

Les Etrusques et l'Europe, exhibition cat., Paris and Milan 1992.

Angiolo Fabbrichesi, *Guida della Galleria Buonarroti*, Florence 1865.

Amelio Fara, "Michelangelo e l'architettura militare," in *Atti del Convegno di Studi "Architettura militare nell'Europa del XVI secolo,"* edited by Carlo Cresti, Amelio Fara, and Daniela Lamberini, exhibition cat., Siena 1988.

Flavio Fergonzi, in *Michelangelo nell'Ottocento. Rodin e Michelangelo*, edited by Maria Mimita Lamberti and Christopher Riopelle, exhibition cat., Casa Buonarroti, Milan 1996.

Giovan Battista Fidanza, *Vincenzo Danti 1530–1576*, Florence 1996.

Gigliola Fragnito, *In museo e in villa. Saggi sul Rinascimento perduto*, Venice 1988.

Daniela Gallo, *Filippo Buonarroti e la cultura antiquaria sotto gli ultimi Medici*, exhibition cat., Casa Buonarroti, Florence 1986.

Benvenuto Gasparoni, "La Casa di Michelagnolo Buonarroti," in *Il Buonarroti*, I, 1866.

Il Giardino di San Marco. Maestri e compagni del giovane Michelangelo, edited by Paola Barocchi, exhibition cat., Casa Buonarroti, Milan 1992.

Giorgio Vasari. Principi, letterati e artisti nelle carte di Giorgio Vasari. Pittura vasariana dal 1532 al 1554, exhibition cat., Florence 1981.

Giovanni Volpato 1735–1803, edited by Giorgio Marini, exhibition cat., Bassano 1988.

Alvar Gonzáles-Palacios and François Baratte, *Luigi Valadier au Louvre ou l'Antiquité exaltée*, exhibition cat., Paris 1994.

Aurelio Gotti, *Vita di Michelangelo Buonarroti narrata con l'aiuto di nuovi documenti*, 2 vols., Florence 1875.

Mina Gregori, "Una breve nota su Gregorio Pagani," in *Paragone* 353, 1979.

Michael Hirst, "Addenda Sansoviniana," in *The Burlington Magazine* CXIV, 1972.

————, *Sebastiano del Piombo*, Oxford 1981.

————, *Michelangelo and His Drawings*, New Haven and London 1988.

————, *Michel-Ange dessinateur*, exhibition cat., Paris and Milan 1989.

Indice delle stampe De' Rossi. Contributo alla storia di una Stamperia Romana, edited by Anna Grelle Iusco, Rome 1996.

W. Kamp, *Marcello Venusti. Religiöse Kunst im Umfeld Michelangelos*, Egelsbach 1993.

Paul Marie Letarouilly, *Édifices de Roma Moderne*, 3 vols., Liege 1840–1857.

————, *Le Vatican et la Basilique de Saint-Pierre de Roma*, Paris 1882.

Margrit Lisner, *Il Crocifisso di Michelangelo in Santo Spirito*, Munich 1964.

Pietro C. Marani, *Disegni di fortificazioni da Leonardo a Michelangelo*, exhibition cat., Casa Buonarroti, Florence 1984.

Maria Giovanna Masera, *Michelangelo Buonarroti il Giovane*, Turin 1941.

Michelangelo e il suo mito. Invito in Casa Buonarroti, edited by Pina Ragionieri, exhibition cat., Tokyo 1996.

Michelangelo e la Sistina. La tecnica, il restauro, il mito, exhibition cat., Rome 1990.

Michelangelo entre Florença e Roma. Convite à Casa Buonarroti, edited by Pina Ragionieri, exhibition cat., Florence 1997.

Michelangelo nell'Ottocento. Il centenario del 1875, edited by Stefano Corsi, exhibition cat., Casa Buonarroti, Milan 1994.

Henry A. Millon and Vittorio Magnago Lampugnani, *Rinascimento da Brunelleschi a Michelangelo. La rappresentazione dell'architettura*, exhibition cat., Milan 1994.

Alida Moltedo, *La Sistina riprodotta*, exhibition cat., Rome 1991.

Luisa Morozzi and Rita Paris, *L'opera da ritrovare. Repertorio del patrimonio artistico italiano disperso all'epoca della seconda guerra mondiale*, Rome 1995.

Alessandro Nova, *Michelangelo architetto*, Milan 1984.

L'oro di Valadier. Un genio nella Roma del Settecento, edited by Alvar Gonzáles-Palacios, exhibition cat., Rome 1997.

Gianni Papi, *Il Seicento fiorentino. Arte a Firenze da Ferdinando I a Cosimo III. Disegno/Incisione/Scultura/Art Minori*, exhibition cat., Florence 1986.

———, *Andrea Commodi*, Florence 1994.

Alessandro Parronchi, *Una Ricordanza del Figiovanni sui lavori della Cappella e della Libreria medicee* (1964), in *Opere giovanili di Michelangelo*, Florence 1968.

Claudio Pizzorusso, *Ricerche su Cristofano Allori*, Florence 1982.

J. Graham Pollard, "Il medagliere mediceo," in *Gli Uffizi. Quattro secoli di una galleria*, Atti del Convegno, edited by Paola Barocchi and Giovanna Ragionieri, 2 vols., Florence 1983.

———, *Medaglie italiane del Rinascimento nel Museo Nazionale del Bargello*, III, Florence 1985.

Anny E. Popp, *Die Medici-Kapelle Michelangelos*, Munich 1922.

Ugo Procacci, *La Casa Buonarroti a Firenze*, Milan 1965.

Pina Ragionieri, *Miguel Angel entre Florencia y Roma*, exhibition cat., Valencia 1997.

Rodin and Michelangelo. A Study in Artistic Inspiration, edited by Maria Mimita Lamberti and Christopher Riopelle, exhibition cat., Milan and Philadelphia 1997.

Giuseppe Ignazio Rossi, *La Libreria Mediceo-Laurenziana architettura di Michelagnolo Buonarroti*, Florence 1739.

Fabia Borroni Salvadori, "Le esposizioni d'arte a Firenze dal 1674 al 1767," in *Mitteilungen des Kunsthistorischen Institutes in Florenz*, XVIII, 1974.

San Lorenzo 393–1993. L'architettura. Le vicende della fabbrica, edited by Gabriele Morolli and Pietro Ruschi, exhibition cat., Florence 1993.

Erika Schmidt, in *Vittoria Colonna Dichterin und Muse Michelangelos*, edited by Sylvia Ferino-Padgen, exhibition cat., Vienna 1997.

Ernst Steinmann, *Die Sixtinische Kapelle*, 2 vols., Munich 1901–1905.

———, *Die Portraitdarstellungen des Michelangelo*, Leipzig 1913.

Fiorenza Vannel and Giuseppe Toderi, *La medaglia barocca in Toscana*, Florence 1987.

Benedetto Varchi, "Lezzione nella cuale si disputa della maggioranza delle arti (1546)," in *Trattati d'arte del Cinquecento fra manierismo e controriforma*, edited by Paola Barocchi, 3 vols., Bari 1960.

Claudio Varese, "Teatro, prosa, poesia," in *Il Seicento*, Milan 1967.

Giorgio Vasari, *La vita di Michelangelo nelle redazioni del 1550 e del 1568*, edited and with commentary by Paola Barocchi, 5 vols., Milan and Naples 1962.

———, *Le vite de' più eccellenti pittori, scultori e architettori*, edited by Paola Barocchi and Rosanna Bettarini, 7 vols., Florence 1967–1987.

Massimo Vezzosi, in *Arte in Toscana dal XV al XVIII secolo. Dipinti, disegni, sculture presentati da Massimo Vezzosi*, Florence 1995.

Johannes Wilde, "Due bozzetti di Michelangelo ricomposti," in *Dedalo*, VIII, 1928.

———, "Zwei Modelle Michelangelos für das Julius-Grabmal," in *Jahrbuch der Kunsthistorischen Sammlungen in Wien*, N.F., II, 1928.

———, "Eine Studie Michelangelos nach der Antike," in *Mitteilungen des Kunsthistorischen Institutes in Florenz*, IV, 1932–1934.

———, "Michelangelo's Designs for the Medici Tombs," in *Journal of the Warburg and Courtauld Institutes*, XVIII, 1955.

———, "Notes on the Genesis of Michelangelo's 'Leda,'" in *Fritz Saxl 1890–1948. A Volume of Memorial Essays from His Friends in England*, edited by D. J. Gordon, London 1957.

———, *Michelangelo, Six Lectures*, Oxford 1978.

Hellmut Wohl, "Two Cinquecento Puzzles," in *Antichità viva*, XXX, 1991.